Roll Back the Stone

Roll Back the Stone

Death and Burial in the World of Jesus

Byron R. McCane

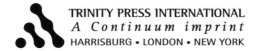

TRINITY PRESS INTERNATIONAL
A Continuum imprint
HARRISBURG • LONDON • NEW YORK

Trinity Press International, P.O. Box 1321, Harrisburg, PA 17105
Trinity Press International is a member of the Continuum International Publishing Group.

Cover art: *The Resurrection: The Angel Rolling Away the Stone from the Sepulchre,* William Blake. Copyright Victoria & Albert Museum, London/Art Resource, N.Y.

Cover design: Tara Shuler

Library of Congress Cataloging-in-Publication Data
McCane, Byron R.
    Roll back the stone : death and burial in the world of Jesus / Byron R. McCane.
        p. cm.
Includes index.
    ISBN 1-56338-402-7 (pbk.)
        1. Funeral rites and ceremonies—Palestine—History. 2. Jesus Christ—Burial.
3. Palestine—Social life and customs. 4. Palestine—History—70-638. I. Title.

GT3274.5.P19 M33 2003
393.9'095694—dc21   2002153968

Printed in the United States of America

03 04 05 06 07 08 09   10 9 8 7 6 5 4 3 2 1

Contents

Acknowledgments

Every book is an admission of ignorance, and never was that more true than in this case. The work presented here began in a fit of curiosity aroused by ignorance, proceeded through confusion and doubt, and has ended in fascination. That journey has been shared by friends, colleagues, and loved ones along the way, and in this brief note I want to express to them my thanks. I am blessed to know some pretty remarkable people in this world, people who also happen to be very, very bright. Henry Carrigan at Trinity Press International is a patient editor who truly understands the hopes which beat in the heart of an academic, and Amy Wagner displayed a gentle firmness that left me no choice but to remain on schedule. Eric Meyers, my principal mentor in all things archaeological, first encouraged me to pursue this topic, and he has taught me more than I can remember. Without the kind assistance of Levi Rahmani, Rachel Hachlili, and Joe Zias at the very beginning, this project might never have gotten off the ground. Colleagues from several seasons of excavations at Sepphoris and Khirbet Cana have enriched my thinking (and eating and drinking and living) in ways they probably never realized. Countless conversations around the dig helped give shape to many of the ideas in this book, and all of the following friends might be able to recognize their own contribution here and there: Carol Meyers, Jonathan Reed, Milton Moreland, Melissa Aubin, Alysia Fischer, J. P. Dessel, Mark Chancey, Jürgen Zangenberg, Greg Smith, Bill Grantham, Stuart Miller, Doug Edwards, Jack Olive, Peter Richardson, Aaro Söderlund, Doug Oakman, and Erin Roberts. Closer to home, a debt of gratitude goes to my daughters, Julie and Laura, who may find in these pages the reason why their dad's job is so different from their friends' dads' jobs. But most of all I am grateful to Linda, who made room in her life for a husband who likes to go halfway around the world to play in the dirt. She is an artist, and from her I have learned that there comes a time when you have to put down the brush and hang your painting where someone can see it.

Introduction:
Death as a Fact of Life

It must have been a *very* unusual funeral. A rabbi of the stature of Gamaliel II—president of the Sanhedrin, head of the academy at Javneh, and emissary to the emperor in Rome—ought to have been carried out to his tomb in a grand procession and with splendid adornments. Certainly that was what the mourners gathered for his funeral that day in the early second century had every reason to expect, since recent funerals in Palestine had featured increasingly elaborate displays of wealth, with corpses dressed in expensive garments of linen and wool. Some people were even beginning to joke that the burden of *clothing* the dead could hit a family harder than the death itself. Surely Rabban Gamaliel's funeral would surpass them all. It did not work out that way, however. Unbeknownst to the waiting mourners, the rabbi had quietly arranged in advance to make an example of himself. "Disregarding his own dignity," as the Babylonian Talmud puts it, he had left instructions for his body to be prepared for burial in the most humble attire. And so it happened that when the body of Gamaliel II was carried to its final resting place, it was wrapped not in fine linen or wool, but in plain ordinary flax. The point of this gesture was not lost on the audience, and the reaction was just what the rabbi had hoped for: from that day forward, "the people followed his lead to carry out the dead in flaxen vestments" (*t. Mo'ed Qat.* 27b).

Rabban Gamaliel had hit upon an important fact about funerals, namely, that they are deeply social events. When human beings assemble in groups to lay a corpse to rest, a complex array of social and cultural interactions begins to take place. This is a book about those interactions, or at least about those that took place when the people of early Roman Palestine gathered to bury their dead. This

1

is a book, that is, about funerary practice at the eastern end of the
Mediterranean between 63 B.C.E. and 135 C.E. The aim of this book
is to observe and analyze the ways in which the death ritual of
early Roman Palestine adjudicated social conflicts, celebrated cultural ideals, and established a social structure. This region and
period has long been of interest to historians and scholars of religion because it was the homeland not only of Gamaliel II but also
of the historical Jesus, and the birthplace of both Judaism and
Christianity. As a result, Roman Palestine now enjoys a prominence in our history books that it scarcely held in antiquity. During
the first century C.E. a writer such as Pliny the Elder could pass
over it in just a few paragraphs, noting little more than the "pleas-
ant" waters of the Jordan River, the "noxious" fumes of the Dead Sea,
and the "amazing" celibate men of the Essenes (*Nat. Hist.* 5.68–73).
In recent years, by contrast, a steady stream of advanced literary,
historical, and archaeological research has substantially filled out
our picture of that place and time, including not only its natural
geography but also its history, politics, society, and culture.[1] Now
scholars can argue over such detailed issues as whether the cultural and religious heritage of the Galileans was primarily Israelite
or Hasmonean, or whether the celibate men at Qumran even were
Essenes. Despite this considerable body of work, however, the
topic of death ritual has barely been sketched in, and no comprehensive treatment of it has yet been offered. The point of this book
is to begin to fill that gap, and to help us begin to understand the
ways in which the people of early Roman Palestine—including
Gamaliel II, the Galileans, and those "amazing" men at Qumran—
coped with the dark and yet universal fact of human death.[2]

The study of death ritual in early Roman Palestine begins with
what the people of that place and time wrote down on the subject.
Gamaliel II, it turns out, had good reason to fear that his funeral
might become an occasion for status mongering, since competition
for prestige was evidently rather common at funerals in antiquity.
Certainly the rabbi was not the only one to notice it. Josephus
knew of Jewish families who had reduced themselves to poverty by
spending too much on a funeral (*Jewish War* 2.1), and the Babylonian
Talmud mentions that some families, faced with their inability to
provide an impressive funeral, chose instead simply to abandon
their loved one's remains (*b. Mo'ed Qat.* 27b). Probably few families

actually went so far as to take such drastic steps, but texts like these do show that the people of early Roman Palestine were consciously aware of the financial costs and social benefits of a splendid funeral. And they were not the only ones. In Greece and Rome, both Solon and Cicero had strongly condemned ostentatious death ritual, levying fines against those who indulged in what they regarded as excessive displays of wealth and grief. To Cicero the problem was moral—differences in wealth, he argued, ought to end at death—while Solon feared that grieving women might express themselves in ways that would violate the limits of propriety (Cicero, *Leg.* 2.23.59–24.60; Plutarch, *Solon* 21.6). Even Plato had acknowledged that there was popular esteem for a "magnificent burial" (*megaloprepēs taphē*; *Hippias major* 291d). Among the ancients—whether Greek, Roman, or Jewish—the competition for status stretched all the way from the cradle to the grave, a fact of life (and death) of which they were all too aware. A number of ancient writers actually worried that some funerals might be entirely for show. Lucian, in a biting satire on traditional Greek funerals, sarcastically asserted that mourners were simply performing for an audience (*De luctu* 15), and Pliny the Younger complained that the relatives of one deceased youth were not truly grieving but just showing off.[3] The funeral of a prominent senator, by contrast, he regarded as a ceremony that did "credit to the emperor and our times, to the forum and its speakers."[4] In a similar vein Josephus passes along the accusation that Archelaus's grief after the death of his father Herod was "a sham," since the son reportedly mourned by day while indulging in drunken orgies by night (*Jewish War* 2.1). Living in and shaped by societies that were intensely preoccupied with position, status, and wealth, the ancients could spot a social performance when they saw one, even at the cemetery.

Detecting elements of hypocrisy in death ritual, however, is rather like seeing the tip of an iceberg—much more is there than meets the eye. It was not so easy for the men and women of antiquity to recognize the more subtle social and cultural transactions that were taking place in and through their death ritual. For that reason this book will also make use of theory from sociology and anthropology in order to analyze aspects of ancient death ritual of which the participants themselves may not have been consciously aware. A few ancient writers did sense that funerals could have a broader social purpose. Augustine, for one, wrote that "all of these things—funeral arrangements, tomb preparations, solemn processions—are more to comfort the living than to help the dead" (*De cura pro mortuis gerenda* 4). Such a remark might seem like a commonplace, but it is not a truism to observe that one of the social purposes of a funeral is to offer a specific kind of solace to the survivors. Funeral rituals almost always include verbal and/or symbolic expressions of assurance that life will go on. Robert Hertz, whose 1907 monograph "Contribution à une étude sur la représentation collective de la mort" was one of the earliest modern studies of death ritual, understood the social force of such representations. Hertz wrote that death does much more than merely end the biological life of an individual person: it also affects an entire social group, striking that group "in the very principle of its life, in the faith it has in itself."[5] By this he meant that human death, by forcibly removing a member of a social network, calls into question the ongoing viability of the network as a whole. The removal of one individual is an attack upon the entire social organism, and the more prominent the member affected, the more dangerous the attack is felt to be. From this (functionalist) sociological perspective Hertz regarded death ritual as a social event that meets the threat of death head on, ensuring that in the ongoing argument between life and death, life will always get the last word. Through death ritual the social network—and the men and women of antiquity can hardly have been expected to have noticed this—is repaired and reconstructed. Social structure is established through death ritual, in other words, and if we hope to understand the social structure of early Roman Palestine, a study of death ritual will be indispensable.

Rabban Gamaliel's choice of burial attire shows that he understood something else about death ritual as well, namely, its cultural power. Certainly death ritual has the potential to influence and shape those who witness and participate in it, a fact that Gamaliel exploited to advantage. By planning in advance, he was able to arrange for the appearance of his corpse to have the impact of reversing a prevailing social and cultural trend. Anxiously awaited by the assembled mourners, the flaxen-shrouded body of the rabbi instantly constituted itself into a symbol and powerfully inscribed itself upon the crowd. Mary Douglas and Peter Brown, among others, have shown that marking and display of the human body can symbolically express the social order, and Rabban Gamaliel appears to have sensed that display of a dead human body could accomplish similar ends. Anthropological studies confirm in theory what Gamaliel no doubt understood only by intuition, namely, that the human corpse on ritual display is a cultural symbol of unusual force. "If the human body in life provides such a rich reservoir of moral representations, this same body after death carries its own possibilities for symbolic expression."[6] The people of early Roman Palestine saw corpses on ritual display more often than modern westerners do: the corpse could be seen in the home of the deceased, during the funeral procession, and as it was placed in the tomb. In Jewish death ritual, the corpse became a symbol yet one more time at the ceremony of "secondary burial," when the bones of the corpse were reburied after the flesh of the body had decayed. This Jewish ritual of secondary burial illustrates the cultural power of death ritual particularly well, since the reburial of human bones is a task which—to current Western sensibilities at least—seems highly unpleasant and perhaps also rather time consuming. Yet the Jews of early Roman Palestine did it without flinching or complaining. Secondary burial did not repulse or annoy them because it was replete with symbolic representations of values they held most dear. Even a task like collecting the bones of a desiccated corpse is not offensive if one can see it as an expression of all that makes life good. This study of death ritual in early Roman Palestine, then, will not only clarify the social structure of that place and time; it will also elucidate some of the most fundamental values and norms upon which that culture was based.

In addition to documents from antiquity and theory from anthropology, this book will also make use of what the men and women of early Roman Palestine have left behind in their tombs and graves, that is, the archaeological record of their death ritual. Material culture is an indispensable counterpart to the literary sources because it provides much-needed correction and/or corroboration of the evidence from the texts. Hundreds of tombs and graves from this region and period have been carefully excavated and published, and the funerary archaeology of Roman Palestine now includes not only excavation reports but also secondary analyses of the finds. A few of those finds have been headline grabbers: in 1968 the bones of a crucifixion victim were found at Giv'at ha-Mivtar, and in 1990 a Jerusalem tomb produced an ossuary inscribed with the name "Caiaphas."[7] Such sensational discoveries are rare, of course, and do not represent the value of archaeology for this book. It is not, after all, the dramatic and exceptional discovery that best illumines the customs and conventions of an ancient society and culture, but rather the cumulative impression of many ordinary and typical finds. To that end, this book will make use of a relatively large number of tombs and graves in order to reconstruct the prevalent and conventional death rituals of early Roman Palestine. Of course the archaeological remains will provide some of the most compelling data with which this book will deal, since human skeletons and their accompanying grave goods often evoke unusually vivid impressions of ancient ways of life. Few and far between are those who will not be moved when they read of the female skeleton at Giv'at ha-Mivtar, which was found with the remains of a full-term fetus lying amid its pelvic bones.[8] A tender humanistic empathy is the natural and healthy response to such finds, but that is not the principal value of archaeology in this book. The focus here is on death ritual, that is, the ritual process by which skeletons and grave goods came to be deposited as they were. Even though the condition of this or that particular skeleton or tomb may provide us with moving anecdotes about this or that individual person or family, those anecdotes will not always illumine the social and cultural norms of early Roman Palestine. Individual finds, however eye-catching or heart-stopping they may be, do not necessarily shed light on the conventions and customs of an ancient society. Only a study of how and why human remains came to be deposited as they were can enable us to reconstruct the ritual process of death, and only the ritual process of death can provide the kind of information that we are seeking about the society and culture of early Roman Palestine.

The region and period attract interest not only because of the presence of historical figures like Gamaliel II and Jesus of Nazareth, but also because early Roman Palestine was the setting for a complex confluence of peoples and cultures. The social structure of this place and time was made up of Jews, Greeks, and Romans, all living and dying in close proximity to each other. Under the auspices of Roman political and military authority, the cultural streams of Judaism and Hellenism encountered and came to terms with each other in creative ways. Long-standing ancient Near Eastern cultural traditions were forced to adapt to and coexist with more recent Greek and Roman arrivals from the West. The temple in Jerusalem exemplifies many of the contours of this coexistence. Its architectural style was Hellenistic, with colonnades and porticoes, and it was built by Herod the Great, a client of Rome, but the religious rituals performed there were Jewish, with roots in the priestly traditions of Israelite religion. Similar confluences of Judaism and Hellenism can be seen in the death ritual of early Roman Palestine as well. The so-called *loculus* niche, for example, a deep narrow niche carved into the wall of a tomb, large enough to hold one body, was a Hellenistic development that first appeared in Palestine at Maresha during the second century B.C.E. But these niches rapidly became very popular, and by the middle of the first century C.E. they had become the most widely used burial niche in Palestine. Jewish families often used them for secondary burial, thereby taking a Hellenistic burial niche and making it the setting for a traditional Jewish custom. Other Hellenistic influences are also evident. At Beth She'arim in the Lower Galilee, a large complex of catacombs was used for the burial of Jews from Palestine and the Diaspora during the second through fourth centuries C.E. Among the most impressive of these catacombs are 12 and 14, each of which has a monumental entrance with a triple archway, a typical example of Roman architectural style. Inside the catacombs at Beth She'arim, most of the burial niches are *arcosolia*, that is, arch-shaped recesses of Hellenistic design.[9] The interior walls, however, bear inscriptions not only in Greek but also in Hebrew. This interplay of Jewish and Hellenistic elements is especially important because Catacomb 14 served as the final resting place of Rabbi Judah ha-Nasi, the compiler of the Mishnah. The rabbi's burial place provides a vivid microcosm of broader cultural movements underway during his lifetime. No doubt the ritual process by which his body was laid to rest in that burial place must have reflected the interplay of Judaism and Hellenism as well. This study of death ritual in early Roman Palestine, in other words, is more than just a survey of burial practices: it is also a case study in the ancient conversation between Judaism and Hellenism.

Despite the fact that Jews, Greeks, and Romans were all living and dying in the same region at the eastern end of the Mediterranean between 63 B.C.E. and 135 C.E., the cultural traditions of Israel, Greece, and Rome did not deal with the end of human life in the same way. Of course there were similarities, such as the fact that Jews and pagans carried their dead out to the place of interment in a funerary procession, but a passerby watching a funeral procession in Caesarea, Jerusalem, or Sepphoris would have had little difficulty in recognizing whether the deceased was Jewish or Greek. There were simply too many differences. Greeks and Romans put their corpses on public display in ways that attempted to make them appear lifelike, but Jews generally took few if any steps to conceal the mortality of the deceased. Greeks and Romans mourned the dead for several days; Jews mourned their dead for a full year. And only Jews practiced secondary burial. Despite many similarities and small shades of difference, then, the death ritual of early Roman Palestine can still be broadly classified into two recognizable forms, one Jewish and one pagan, and characteristic differences can be observed between them. Jewish death ritual had its roots in ancient Near Eastern customs that reached as far back as the late Chalcolithic Age (ca. 3800–3400 B.C.E.), when inhabitants of the Levant first began to bury their dead by family groups in underground tombs. The custom of secondary burial, so prevalent among Jews in early Roman Palestine, went back to the late Bronze Age, when tribes and clans first began to pile the bones of their ancestors on one side of their underground burial chambers. These ancient customs had already undergone significant changes by the time first Hellenism and then the Roman Empire arrived in Palestine before the turn of the era. The simple, round, late Bronze Age underground chamber, for example, in which bones were piled to one side, had developed into the so-called "bench" tomb of the Iron Age, in which benches ran along the sides of a square chamber and bones were collected in recesses beneath the benches.

The arrival of Greeks and Romans in Palestine did not cause traditional Jewish customs to disappear, then, but only to change yet again, as cultural influences from areas outside the Near East increasingly came into play. Greek and Roman burial customs had their roots in archaic Greek practices and, in the case of Rome, in Etruscan antecedents. There the dominant pattern of burial had been the use of stone sarcophagi in multi-chambered underground tombs, and, in many cases, cremation and burial in urns or pots.[10]

In response to these new and foreign cultural influences, the Jews of early Roman Palestine adapted new methods of practicing their ancestral rites. The rise of the Jewish ossuary is but one of many examples. Unlike previous generations, which had piled bones on one side of the tomb (late Bronze Age) or gathered them into recesses in a "bench tomb" (Iron Age), Jews in early Roman Palestine, especially in the vicinity of Jerusalem, now collected the bones of their dead in small limestone chests, or ossuaries. The rise of ossuaries, bone containers that preserved the identity of the deceased, represented a Jewish adaptation of ancient ancestral traditions to newer Hellenistic cultural trends. Secondary burial still went on in hellenized early Roman Palestine, then, as it had in Bronze and Iron Age Palestine, but in ways that differed from the rites of earlier generations in preceding centuries.

In the encounter between Judaism and Hellenism there was no doubt about which culture would be dominant. Hellenism was a world culture, and its introduction into Palestine had begun centuries before the conquests of Alexander, when traders and mercenaries from the Aegean first made their way to Palestine, bringing with them black-figured wares and Attic coins that regularly surface in Persian period strata of archaeological excavations in Israel today. By the middle of the fifth century B.C.E., long before Alexander set foot in Palestine, "the handwriting was already on the wall, and it was in Greek."[11] Yet the intersection between Judaism and Hellenism cannot be viewed as a simple collision or clash in which one tradition "won" while the other "lost," as if Hellenism somehow completely penetrated and overwhelmed the traditional cultures of Syro-Palestine. On the contrary, these traditional cultures showed considerable strength and resilience in the face of Hellenism, and Jews in particular exercised a high degree of selectivity and creativity in their appropriation of it. In Palestine, as elsewhere, Hellenism did not so much extinguish traditional local ways of life as it provided new outlets for the expression of indigenous norms and values.[12]

Certainly this was the case with Jewish death ritual, where Jews made free and extensive use of some Hellenistic elements, but at the same time they also found new ways to transform and continue ancient traditions. Rituals of death and burial, in fact, are typically among the more conservative and stable elements in a society,

changing very slowly over generations and centuries. The death
ritual of early Roman Palestine fits this general pattern. Jews did
not immediately respond to the arrival of Hellenism with a wholesale overhaul of their traditional burial customs. Some forms of
Hellenistic tomb architecture—the *loculus* niche, for example—did
spread quite rapidly through Palestine, but most traditional Jewish
death ritual remained relatively stable during the early Roman
period. The dead were still buried as they long had been: promptly,
and by family groups in underground caves. Those caves were still
located a safe distance away from the boundaries of human habitation in the community. During the procession that carried the
corpse to the tomb, there was no effort to make the corpse appear
lifelike, and the principal participants in the burial ceremony were
still the closest members of the immediate family. And those same
family members still returned to the tomb to gather the bones of
the dead after the flesh of the body had decayed. There was, in
other words, a well-established pattern of death ritual in early
Roman Palestine, with deep roots in ancient Near Eastern custom,
and few highly dramatic departures from it took place during the
early Roman period. The social structure of early Roman Palestine
was not shifting around dramatically.

But it *was* shifting, slowly at first, under the immense weight of
great cultural and political pressures from the West. The long-
standing ancient Near Eastern pattern of burial practices, deeply
rooted though it was, could not stand indefinitely against the constant force of Hellenistic and Roman influence. In the specific area
of death ritual, two particular changes betray the strength of those
influences. First, Hellenism brought to the land of Israel the idea
that the individual identity of the deceased should be preserved
after death. Greeks and Romans had long protected the identity of
the individual deceased, so that even though they buried their dead
in various ways—in sarcophagi, or in *arcosolium* or *loculus* niches
within underground chambers, or even in shaft graves—all of
these various means of interment still had the effect of preserving
the individual identity of human remains. Even when the dead
were cremated, their ashes were customarily gathered up and disposed of individually. This kind of attention to individual identity
after death was quite in keeping with the prominence of the individual human being in Hellenistic law, philosophy, art, literature,

and religion, but it was very different from the traditional Israelite emphasis on family, tribe, and clan. Ancient Israelite religion and culture had always placed more emphasis on the group than on the individual, and this emphasis found vivid ritual expression in the practice of collective secondary burial. From the simple underground chambers of the Chalcolithic Age to the chiseled bench tombs of the Iron Age and then the charnel rooms of the late Hellenistic period, the ultimate destiny of the deceased was to be gathered into a heap along with all those who had gone before. Among the Israelites, bone-gathering of this sort had given rise to the recurrent biblical expression, "he slept and was gathered to his fathers," and once the remains of an Israelite had been "gathered to his fathers," those remains were forever indistinguishable from the remains of the fathers. The identity of the individual deceased was completely dissolved into an ancestral collective. During the early Roman period, however, Jews in Palestine (especially in and around Jerusalem) began to preserve the identity of individuals after death. They still gathered bones, but now they put them in ossuaries and inscribed those ossuaries with the names of the deceased. Rather than being lost among the ancestors, the identity of the deceased was preserved even after secondary burial. This departure from tradition is best explained by the rising influence of Hellenistic cultural ideals that valorized the individual human being.

In addition, the arrival of Greeks and Romans in Palestine gave fresh momentum to a set of practices that had persisted for centuries at the popular level even though they had repeatedly been condemned by Israelite and Jewish religious authorities. I refer here to practices in which the living continued to have contact with the dead, in body or in spirit, even after burial. Rituals of this sort were a standard and accepted practice in the Hellenistic world, where death and burial did not bring to an end the social connection between the living and the dead. On the contrary, relatives and friends of the deceased met regularly at the burial site for memorial meals known as *refrigeria*, festive occasions that were thought to be "refreshing" for all concerned, including the deceased. Among the Greeks the first of these gatherings was held on the third day after death, followed by additional visits on the ninth and thirtieth days, and still later by monthly and annual commemorative gatherings at the grave.[13] Romans likewise gathered at the burial place

on the ninth day after death to celebrate the *cena novendialis*, and
then observed an "annual official commemoration of the dead" in
late February known as the *Parentalia* or *dies Parentales*.[14] Feasting
with the dead was, in other words, an ordinary and typical feature
of life in Greek and Roman society.

Ongoing contact between the living and the dead was known,
but frequently condemned, in Jewish tradition. During the biblical
period a cult of the dead was thriving at the popular level in Israel.
Elizabeth Bloch-Smith has offered the most thorough treatment of
that cult, and her review of the archaeological and biblical evidence
shows that Israelites regularly offered food to the dead and consulted with them on matters of fortune-telling and divination.[15]
But Israelite religious authorities actively resisted this cult and
took steps to try to stamp it out. Bloch-Smith traces this opposition
through the biblical text and locates its origin during the eighth and
seventh centuries among "palace and Jerusalem Temple Yahwistic
cult authorities."[16] This early official opposition became the foundation for Jewish disapproval of gatherings in the presence of the dead.
In Num 19:11–22, for example, corpses are declared to be ritually
impure, and contact with the dead is said to render one unfit to
enter the sanctuary of the temple. Over the ensuing centuries, as
developments in post-biblical Judaism made the Torah increasingly central to Jewish civilization, the opinions of the eighth-
century palace elite came to acquire a heftier cultural weight. By
the time of the Roman Empire, many Jews were actively avoiding
unnecessary contact with tombs and the dead, especially around
the time of holidays and festivals. Pharisees in particular seem to
have been especially concerned to avoid contracting ritual impurity from corpses, graves, or tombs. At the same time, however,
some kind of cult of the dead was certainly still going on among
Jews in early Roman Palestine. The archaeological evidence plainly
shows as much: cooking pots are one of the most common types
of pottery typically found in Jewish tombs of this region and
period. Someone (most likely members of the immediate family)
was bringing food to the dead. The persistence of such activities in
the face of a strong Jewish cultural tradition against them hints at
the social and religious power that infused this secret contact with
the dead. Always at the margin and ever potentially dangerous,
the Jewish dead nonetheless could be seen as valued mentors and

silent conversation partners. In the Greeks and Romans, then, the Jews of early Roman Palestine encountered peoples who regarded these kinds of meetings with the dead as normal, natural, and good, even refreshing. Offerings of food to the dead were an ordinary part of their daily lives, and they feasted with the dead on a regular basis, in public and without shame. The impact of their practices and attitudes gave fresh momentum to Jewish activities that had long been lurking just below the surface.

Both of these developments in Jewish death ritual—the rise of the ossuary and the strengthening of the cult of the dead—were the result of Hellenistic cultural influences. Both also had a significant, although not immediate, impact on the social structure of early Roman Palestine. Over time they had the effect of redrawing the social boundaries within which people lived and died. In particular, ossuaries and the cult of the dead reconfigured the boundary between those who had died and those who had not, and in so doing altered the terms by which the living and the dead would relate to each other. Every society has to deal with the problem of what to do with a person who has died, and physical disposal of the corpse is only part of the solution. Something must also be done about the social persona of the deceased, the being who has acquired social significance by filling various roles in the social network. A human body that ceases its biological functioning does not merely die; it also brings to an end the existence of a social persona—a parent, a child, an uncle, an aunt, a worker, an owner, a member, a neighbor, a friend. As Robert Hertz put it, "Death does not confine itself to ending the visible daily life of an individual; it also destroys the social being grafted onto the physical individual, to whom the collective consciousness attributed importance."[17] Jewish society in early Roman Palestine had inherited a well-established ritual process with which to handle this problem. Through the rituals of death and secondary burial, the deceased were symbolically removed from the social order of the living and placed into the company of the dead, where they took their place in a separate society, distinct from the one populated by the living. When the ceremonies of burial were complete, the social persona of the deceased had been extinguished, his or her bones had been gathered into the ancestors, and he or she no longer belonged to the social order of the living. The rite of secondary burial symbolically represented this extinction in an especially vivid way by ritually dissolving the body of the deceased into the collective heap of the bones of all those who had gone before. In those vivid words of the Israelite texts, the deceased was "gathered to the fathers."

The rise of the ossuary—an individual container for secondary burial—marked a change in this social structure because it preserved the identity of the individual deceased even after death and secondary burial. With the use of an individual burial container, the identity of the deceased did not disappear into the mass of an ancestral collective, but remained as distinct and clear as the name of the individual inscribed on the ossuary. In so doing, the social persona of the deceased was preserved, a fact that is particularly evident in ossuary inscriptions. These inscriptions, which may appear almost anywhere on an ossuary, serve to identify the individual whose bones are collected within. As such they almost always mention the name of the deceased. Often, however, they also include epithets describing his or her social persona. Family relationships, for example, "are referred to in about half of the inscriptions mentioning the name of the deceased."[18] Titles, designations, and professions also appear, and when they do they usually mention specific social roles, such as priest, scribe, teacher, or proselyte. Exceptional contributions to Jewish society show up as well, for example in the inscriptions on the ossuaries of "Nicanor, who built the gates of the Temple" and "Simon, builder of the sanctuary."[19] The point here is that the use of an ossuary, especially one with an inscription, preserved the very entities that were effectively extinguished by collective secondary burial: the individual identity and the social persona of the deceased. The ossuary kept the individual identity of the deceased in a specific relationship with the social world of the living.

The cult of the dead made that relationship practical and real. Ossuaries enabled the Jews of early Roman Palestine to locate, identify, and consult with specific particular individuals among the dead. We have precious little information about how the Jewish cult of the dead actually functioned in early Roman Palestine—no literary evidence at all, just those cooking pots, which speak silently of food offerings to the dead. But a look around in a typical Jewish tomb from this period leaves a vivid impression. The Kidron Valley tomb reported on by Nahman Avigad in 1962 can serve as a representative illustration.[20] On a shelf that ran along three walls of the rectangular chamber (3.1 m x 4.65 m) Avigad found scattered human bones, and on one side (to the left of the entrance) were ten ossuaries. Nine of these ossuaries were inscribed, all with names of the deceased. Four inscriptions added a family relation of the deceased ("Sabatis, mother of Damon," for example), and two stated the deceased's place of origin ("Sara, daughter of Simon, of Ptolemais"). Several perfume bottles lay on the floor, and a lamp and two cooking pots were found on the shelves along the walls. With just a little imagination, we can reconstruct the process by which those cooking pots came to be deposited in this tomb. During the first century C.E., the scattered bones along the shelves would have been the bodies of family members who had recently died, in varying states of decomposition and not yet gathered into ossuaries. To the left were the ossuaries of family members whose bones had already been gathered, among them Sara, the daughter of Simon, and Alexander, the son of Simon. Into this setting, in which the social ties of family and place were still clearly in evidence, came a Jewish son or grandson, daughter or granddaughter, to consult with the dead. Not much more than a stone's throw from the temple, whose priestly authorities would surely have frowned at the thought of it, he or she brought a food offering to the dead. Cooking pot in one hand and perfume bottle in the other (to relieve the nostrils of the rancid stench inside the tomb), that Jewish son or daughter consulted not an indiscriminate collective heap of bones, but a gathering of individuals whose identities were remembered and whose relationships with the living had not been effaced. The cooking pot, placed on the shelf near the bones of a recently deceased family member, symbolically represented the ongoing connection between living and dead.

In family burial caves like this Kidron Valley tomb, many Jews in early Roman Palestine did as their Israelite ancestors had done, and as they knew Greeks and Romans were still doing. In private darkness, hidden from the disapproving eyes of priests and Pharisees, they quietly consulted with their dead. The public authorities may have tried to assert that the social structure of Jewish culture should not include the dead, but the reality of ordinary life had a secret place for them. Perhaps it was inevitable that in time these private practices would eventually have an impact on the social

structure in ways that would become public and visible. Much
later, as Hellenistic norms of individual identity and communion
with the dead came to be complemented by cultural developments
during the Byzantine period, one sect within Judaism finally took
the step of going public with its cult of the dead. Linking their own
distinctive religious beliefs with Greek and Roman cultural mores,
and drawing upon the same social and cultural energies that had
fueled the secret Jewish cult of the dead for centuries, the members
of this sect began to distinguish themselves from other Jews
through the public practice of ritual contact with the dead. The
process unfolded slowly and gradually, but eventually Christians
began to move in the direction of public ritual gatherings in the
presence of the dead. As we have seen, death ritual is intimately
related to social structure, and changes in death ritual usually are
associated with changes in social structure. The emergence of a
public Christian cult of the dead, then, marked the emergence of a
distinctively Christian relationship between the living and the
dead, a relationship in which the Jewish boundary between life and
death was redrawn along Christian parameters. The public
Christian cult of the dead constituted an effort to circumscribe the
grave and the corpse that it contained within an emerging vision
of an ideal Christian society. The fact that the means and inclination to undertake such a project first surfaced among Christians in
Palestine during the late fourth century marks that period as a
watershed in the history of early Judaism and Christianity.

But can a study of death ritual really do all that? Can death ritual
actually produce such significant interpretations of the social
structure of an ancient culture? Perhaps it cannot. Common sense
would seem to suggest that human responses to death are generally similar across different societies and cultures, and that most
cultures respond to death in basically the same way. Death makes
people sad; what could be simpler or more obvious? If that were
true, then death ritual, and the changes therein, would be socially
and culturally insignificant. But it is not true. Human responses to
death actually vary quite dramatically: when human beings assemble in groups to dispose of their dead, a wide range of emotional
and psychological states can ensue, including everything from
rampant sensuality to strict silence. Monica Wilson, for example,
found that the Nyakyusa tribes of Tanzania responded to death

with three days of dancing, feasting, and sex, while Clifford Geertz observed that Javanese funerals were extremely solemn, with even the slightest displays of emotion being strictly proscribed.[21] Most funerals in the western European cultural tradition tend to be rather solemn affairs, but Irish wakes are famous for setting a somewhat more vibrant emotional tone. Psychological responses to death vary across cultures in this way because death ritual is not only, or even primarily, a psychological experience. It is rather a social and cultural event, driven not by the religious or emotional needs of individuals, but by tasks and conflicts that confront the society and culture as a whole.[22] More is at stake in a funeral than simply the emotional or psychological narrative of a particular individual, or even of a family or clan.

As a student of Emile Durkheim, Robert Hertz naturally looked at death ritual from a point of view that was not merely sociological, but, more specifically, functionalist. Durkheim saw society as a living organism which employed various processes (including rituals) for purposes of survival. Death, for Durkheim and the functionalists, wounds the organism; death ritual heals the wound. The benefits of a functionalist social theory of death ritual are readily apparent. It can explain, for example, the impressive fact that death ritual is a virtually universal human phenomenon. Every known culture includes rituals for disposal of the dead; not all cultures *bury* their dead, but all do prescribe a socially preferred treatment of human remains.[23] From a functionalist point of view this fact is to be expected, since funerals are ritual processes that enable a society to survive the threat of death. We should thus expect to find funerals in every society, and we do: the world has yet to see a human society that can willingly let its dead lie where they fall. Functionalist sociology can thus account for death ritual's *universality*. It cannot, however, explain another equally impressive fact about death ritual, namely, its *variety*. For although human beings in all places and times have disposed of their dead through ritual, they appear to have done so in virtually every conceivable manner, shape, and form. When human beings gather in groups to dispose of their dead, a dazzlingly wide range of activities may ensue, involving highly diverse emotional states and widely divergent treatments of the corpse. Humans may be utterly silent at a funeral, or wildly expressive; they may sit and weep, or dance and copulate;

they may bury the corpse, or burn it, or leave it to be eaten by animals and birds, or they may even go so far as to employ elaborate technologies in order to make it appear lifelike and asleep.

Death rituals vary in this way because they are not merely social events; they are cultural symbols as well. The death rituals of a particular society valorize the most basic life values of that culture, and societies construct funerary practices that celebrate the ideals of life that are fundamental to the norms and values of that culture. The Nyakyusa tribes studied by Monica Wilson, for example, greeted death with feasting and sex because vigorous sensuality symbolically represented their ideals of gender norms. Javanese mourners, by contrast, restrained all emotion at death in order to affirm the value their culture placed on *iklas*, or "willed affectlessness." The death rituals of any particular culture are typically replete with symbolic representations of the life values of that culture. Burial practices, in other words, not only function to preserve a social organism, healing the wounds inflicted by death, but are also strategic weapons that societies employ in their war against death. The awful threat of death is staved off through ritual and symbolic celebrations of life. Among the Bara tribes of Madagascar, for example, funerals typically include dancing, singing, feasting, sex, and even cattle wrestling. About halfway through the funeral procession, a herd of cattle is stampeded around the coffin and young Bara men compete to see which of them can leap onto one of the stampeding herd and hold on the longest. This kind of behavior arises from the fact that "they [the Bara] view death as an excess or order upsetting the life-sustaining balance [between order and vitality], and that much of the funeral behavior is an attempt to redress the imbalance through a symbolic increase in vitality."[24] Dancing, singing, feasting, sex, and cattle wrestling represent basic Bara values of life. In order for their society to survive in the face of death, they dispose of their dead in ways that express their best hopes for the living. Rituals of death and burial, then, are culturally specific symbolizations that re-present the culture's most basic norms and values for life. Death ritual, in other words, is an artifact of culture.

Plainly then the death ritual of early Roman Palestine can be an avenue through which to explore the social and cultural boundaries of that time and place—in fact, it may be one of the best possible

such avenues. Too many theories about early Roman Palestine
have been based solely on literary sources which speak largely
about theological topics and which have a strong polemical agenda
against an opponent.[25] Some studies of Judaism and Christianity in
early Roman Palestine, for example, focus upon the sharp conflict
between Jews and Christians that is evident in many literary
sources. Certainly from an early date Jews and Christians did criti-
cize and even curse each other, but theories based solely on such
texts overlook the fact that rival groups within the same society
and culture can vilify each other in word and script without frac-
turing the social and cultural order. In American political circles,
Democrats and Republicans routinely condemn each other's ideas,
policies, programs, motives, character, and even personal lives, yet
no one would suggest that such rhetoric signifies that either party
has withdrawn from the American political system. The political
and social alignments of American society are more subtle than
that, and so were the religious, social, and cultural interrelation-
ships within early Roman Palestine. This fact is plainly evident in
the archaeological remains. In the residential neighborhood of
Sepphoris, for example, which was excavated by the Sepphoris
Regional Project, streets laid out on a *Roman* grid were lined with
houses laid out on a traditional *Palestinian* floor plan and decorated
with frescoed walls and mosaic floors. The private areas of these
houses featured *Jewish* ritual baths, and in the food preparation
areas scarcely any pork bones have been found. Somewhere along
these streets there lived at least a few *Christians* as well, but we cannot now tell exactly where because whatever theological and religious disagreements there might have been between Jews and
Christians, they did not produce the kind of social and cultural differences that can be detected in material remains. Thus the obvious
fact that Christians and Jews argued with each other over theological issues should not be allowed to obscure the equally obvious, and
more important, fact that they also shared broad areas of society
and culture in common. The study of death ritual in early Roman
Palestine will not fall prey to the difficulties that have beset studies based solely on literary sources, since death ritual is not essentially a matter of sectarian or theological dispute.

Of course the evidence of texts is still important, and theological
issues are still significant. But the social and cultural boundaries of

early Roman Palestine cannot be traced without the use of both archaeological and literary sources, and without attention to issues that are genuinely social and cultural. Archaeologists, historians, and biblical scholars have made significant progress in the recent past, and many of the details of a productive and reliable method have already been worked out. Certainly it is now widely agreed that archaeology and literature must and can work together, for "text and spade" are mutually interpreting sources of information. Gone are the days when the history of Roman Palestine, or even the history of Jesus of Nazareth, could be written without reference to material culture. As long ago as E. R. Goodenough's pioneering work on Jewish symbols, but especially with the field excavations of E. M. Meyers and J. F. Strange, the influence of archaeology has steadily increased, and current discussions now almost always include a material component.[26] The point, however, is not to employ archaeology merely as a device for "proving" the reliability of a text, nor even to use texts as a means for clarifying difficult archaeological finds, but rather to use both material and literary evidence as equally important sources of historical information. At times, for example, material evidence will govern literature by confirming, supplementing, or even contradicting the assertions of texts. In particular, archaeological remains can preserve direct evidence of an ancient society's typical customs and conventions, against the background of which the ideological agenda of a literary text can stand out more clearly. Yet literary sources can also interpret archaeology by providing background that is not explicit in the material remains, or by helping to shed light upon puzzling finds. Using both material and textual evidence together, the ultimate goal is to arrive at a well-attested reconstruction of history that builds on all the available evidence. To that end, this book will place particular emphasis on those points at which the testimonies of texts and monuments coincide, since historical conclusions based on such intersections can reasonably be regarded as more firmly established.[27]

There is a place for theory in this enterprise as well, especially theory from sociology and anthropology. For as we have already seen, critical analysis of death ritual can produce productive results. Yet the use of theory is not without its problems. Occasionally in the historical study of early Roman Palestine a theory from another

discipline—usually sociology or anthropology, but often economics and politics—is adopted uncritically, or perhaps even wholesale,
without sufficient regard to whether that theory is truly applicable
to conditions in early Roman Palestine. Studies of the historical
Jesus, for example, sometimes construct a vision of the social world
of first-century Galilee on the basis of social, economic, and political theories drawn from the history of medieval Europe. J. Andrew
Overman has catalogued a series of books and articles in which we
can read that Jesus was a peasant who lived in constant tension
with the nearby city of Sepphoris, amid a politics dominated by tax
resentment and the bitterness of lower classes exploited by powerful elites.[28] A closer look at early Roman Galilee, however, serves
to show that such simple and direct application of a theory from
another discipline can be substantially misleading. The economic
relationships between Sepphoris and the surrounding villages do
not actually fit a model of parasitism, in which the city lived off the
productivity of its neighbors. On the contrary, the relationships
appear to have been symbiotic, with both city and towns realizing
economic benefit from their mutual interconnections and interde-
pendence. Villagers marketed their products and services in the
city, as exemplified by the villages of Kefar Ḥananya and Shikhin,
whose pottery wares were sold and used not only in Sepphoris but
across the Lower Galilee.[29] Tensions may have been present among
the towns and villages around Sepphoris, then, but they were not
the tensions of medieval Europe, and the thoughts, feelings, and
motives of first-century Galileans cannot be deduced from the
experiences of medieval Europeans. In the same way that archaeology and literature are best used in complement with each other,
theories from anthropology and sociology function best when they
are allowed to work in tandem with the evidence. While using
anthropological and sociological theory, then, in this book I will
work to keep in view the distinctive circumstances of life and death
in early Roman Palestine. Certainly there will be points of contact
between the death rituals of that place and time and those of other
societies and cultures, and these points of contact will be explored.
But there will be differences as well, and the differences will be
investigated too.

Each of the following chapters will explore one or more aspects
of this development. Chapter 1 outlines the burial practices that

were typical in Palestine during the time period between 63 B.C.E. and 135 C.E., arguing that during this period there were close and deep resonances between Jewish and Christian death ritual. Christians and Jews in early Roman Palestine in fact appear to have shared a common ethnicity. This point will be expanded upon in two subsequent chapters: first a close reading of Q material on the subject of death and burial in chapter 2, and second a historical evaluation of the earliest Christian reports about the burial of Jesus in chapter 3. In each case it will be argued that, when it came to matters of death ritual, Christians in early Roman Palestine were ordinary and typical Jews. The two final chapters will open up the important question of changes in Jewish and Christian burial practices during the early Byzantine period, when differences between Christians and Jews at last began to surface. As we will see in chapter 4, corpse impurity—a cultural norm that early Roman Jews and Christians had held in common—eventually became a point of disagreement and mutual self-definition. The appearance of a Christian identity in the cemetery, I will suggest, coincides with broader social and cultural developments in the late Roman and early Byzantine periods. Finally, chapter 5 will explore the Christian appropriation of images of paradise in ways that completed both their embrace of Hellenistic ritual practices and their adaptation of Jewish traditions. Full consideration of all these matters will have to wait until after the archaeological and textual evidence has been evaluated, but already there is good reason to suspect that the ritual practice of death and burial among Jews and Christians in early Roman Palestine was driven not so much by theological disputes about death and the afterlife as by the steady pressure of larger and more slowly moving social and cultural forces. The fact of human death is after all a profoundly down-to-earth problem, the resolution of which has never been left solely to heaven's jurisdiction.

Notes to Introduction

1. The literature is substantial. Among the most important recent works are: Jonathan L. Reed, *Archaeology and the Galilean Jesus: A Re-examination of the Evidence* (Harrisburg, Penn.: Trinity Press International, 2000); K. C.

Hanson and D. Oakman, *Palestine in the Time of Jesus: Social Structures and Social Conflicts* (Minneapolis: Fortress, 1998); R. A. Horsley, *Archaeology, History, and Society in Galilee: The Social Context of Jesus and the Rabbis* (Valley Forge, Penn.: Trinity Press International, 1996); Tal Ilan, *Jewish Women in Greco-Roman Palestine: An Inquiry into Image and Status* (Tübingen: Mohr Siebeck, 1995); E. P. Sanders, *Judaism: Practice and Belief* (Valley Forge, Penn.: Trinity, 1992); and S. Freyne, *Galilee, Jesus, and the Gospels: Literary Approaches and Historical Investigations* (Philadelphia: Fortress, 1988).

2. Death ritual has already been studied productively in many cultures and periods. For exemplary work in modern cultures, cf. L. M. Danforth, *The Death Rituals of Rural Greece* (Princeton: Princeton University Press, 1982), and E. M. Ahern, *The Cult of the Dead in a Chinese Village* (Palo Alto, Calif.: Stanford University Press, 1973). For analyses of cultures in various historical periods, including antiquity, cf. P. Aries, *The Hour of Our Death* (New York: Knopf, 1981); R. Garland, *The Greek Way of Death* (Ithaca: Cornell University Press, 1985); C. Gittings, *Death, Burial, and the Individual in Early Modern England* (London: Croom Helm, 1984); D. Kurtz and J. Boardman, *Greek Burial Customs* (London: Thames and Hudson, 1971); I. Morris, *Burial and Ancient Society* (Cambridge: Cambridge University Press, 1987), and *Death-Ritual and Social Structure in Classical Antiquity* (Cambridge: Cambridge University Press, 1992); F. S. Paxton, *Christianizing Death* (Ithaca: Cornell University Press, 1990); and J. M. C. Toynbee, *Death and Burial in the Roman World* (Ithaca: Cornell University Press, 1971).

3. Pliny, *Ep.* 4.2.4. Latin: nec dolor erat ille, sed ostentatio doloris.

4. Pliny, *Ep.* 2.1.6. Latin: huius virir exsequiae magnum ornamentum principi magnum saeculo magnum etiam foro et rostris attulerunt.

5. Robert Hertz, *Death and the Right Hand* (trans. Rodney and Claudia Needham; Aberdeen: The University Press, 1960), 78.

6. P. Metcalf and R. Huntington, *Celebrations of Death: The Anthropology of Mortuary Ritual* (2d ed.; New York: Cambridge University Press, 1992), 71.

7. V. Tzaferis, "Jewish Tombs at and near Giv'at ha-Mivtar, Jerusalem," *Israel Exploration Journal* 20 (1970): 18–32. Z. Greenhut, "The 'Caiaphas' Tomb in North Talpiyot, Jerusalem," *'Atiqot* 21 (1992): 63–71.

8. Tzaferis, "Jewish Tombs," 18–32.

9. N. Avigad, *Catacombs 12–23* (vol. 3 of *Beth She'arim*; Jerusalem: Israel Exploration Society, 1971), 42–65.

10. Garland, *The Greek Way of Death*, 34–37; Toynbee, *Death and Burial*, 48–50.

11. Eric M. Meyers, "The Challenge of Hellenism for Early Judaism and Christianity: Galilee in the First Three Centuries," *Biblical Archaeologist* 55 (1992): 86.

12. G. Bowersock, *Hellenism in Late Antiquity* (Ann Arbor: University of Michigan Press, 1990). Cf. also E. M. Meyers, "Jesus and His Galilean

Context," in *Archaeology and the Galilee: Texts and Contexts in the Graeco-Roman and Byzantine Periods* (eds. D. R. Edwards and C. T. McCollough; USF Studies in the History of Judaism 143; Atlanta: Scholars Press, 1997), 57–66.

13. W. Burkert, *Greek Religion* (trans. J. Raffan; Cambridge, Mass.: Harvard University Press, 1985), 190–94. Garland, *The Greek Way of Death*, 104.

14. Toynbee, *Death and Burial*, 63.

15. Elizabeth Bloch-Smith, *Judahite Burial Practices and Beliefs about the Dead* (JSOTSup 123; Sheffield: Sheffield Academic Press, 1992).

16. Ibid., 132.

17. Hertz, *Death and the Right Hand*, 77.

18. L. Y. Rahmani, *A Catalogue of Jewish Ossuaries in the Collections of the State of Israel* (Jerusalem: Israel Antiquities Authority, 1994), 15.

19. Ibid.

20. N. Avigad, "A Depository of Inscribed Ossuaries in the Kidron Valley," *Israel Exploration Journal* 12 (1962): 1–12.

21. Monica Wilson, *Good Company: A Study of Nyakyusa Age Villages* (London: Oxford University Press, 1951). Clifford Geertz, *The Religion of Java* (New York: Free Press, 1960).

22. For the history of anthropological theories of death and burial, cf. Robert Chapman and Klavs Randsborg, "Approaches to the Archaeology of Death," in *The Archaeology of Death* (eds. R. Chapman, I. Kinnes, and K. Randsborg; Cambridge: Cambridge University Press, 1981), 1–24. For further case studies refuting the notion that death ritual is generated by universal human emotions, cf. Metcalf and Huntington, *Celebrations of Death*, chaps. 1 and 2.

23. Peter J. Ucko, "Ethnography and Archaeological Interpretation of Funerary Remains," *World Archaeology* 1 (1969): 262.

24. Metcalf and Huntington, *Celebrations of Death*, 114.

25. Two studies that exemplify this tendency are James D. G. Dunn, *The Parting of the Ways* (Philadelphia: Trinity Press International, 1991) and Steven D. Wilson, *Related Strangers: Jesus and Christians, 70–170 CE*, (Minneapolis: Fortress Press, 1995). Both are careful and articulate and include insightful observations, but both are also based almost entirely on textual evidence, leading them to the conclusion that Judaism and Christianity had effectively separated from each other by the end of the Bar Kokhba Revolt. Theological disagreements, however, do not necessarily signify social and cultural differentiation. Religion is more than theology, and theological disputes that are evident in literary sources do not establish the existence of distinctions in the social world.

26. E. R. Goodenough, *Jewish Symbols in the Greco-Roman Period* (13 vols.; New York: Pantheon, 1953–66). E. M. Meyers and A. T. Kraabel,

"Archaeology, Iconography, and Nonliterary Written Remains," in *Early Judaism and Its Modern Interpreters* (eds. R. A. Kraft and G. W. E. Nicklesburg; Philadelphia: Fortress, 1986), 175–210. The best recent study is Reed, *Archaeology and the Galilean Jesus*.

27. In this regard the use of both material and literary sources is a necessity in any study on the specific topic of death ritual. A history of funerary practice in any region or period that did not build on both archaeology and literature would simply not be convincing, since archaeological evidence of funerary practice can, on its own, be seriously misleading. Peter J. Ucko in "Ethnography and Archaeological Interpretation of Funerary Remains" and John O'Shea in *Mortuary Variability: An Archaeological Investigation*, (Orlando: Academic Press, 1984) have shown that inescapable vagaries in the preservation of sites can cause crucial data to be permanently lost from our view. Natural decay and destruction, for example, or human intervention (i.e., grave robbing) can obscure the precise contours of the original material culture. In addition, important social aspects of ancient death ritual may have taken forms that were nonmaterial. If social distinctions were displayed only in ritual prayers, for example, or if one social group deposited effects with its corpses, effects that have decayed or been stolen over the centuries, none of the differences would leave any detectable trace in the archaeology of the site. O'Shea has documented this kind of misleading funerary archaeology among the cemeteries of native American tribes in Nebraska and South Dakota. As a result it is imperative that other sources of evidence, particularly texts, be brought into the picture. It was literary sources, in fact, that enabled O'Shea to demonstrate that the funerary archaeology of the native American tribes actually misrepresented their social structure. Hence the double necessity of employing both material and literary evidence in the study of death ritual in Roman Palestine: not only the region and period but also the topic demand it.

28. J. Andrew Overman, "Jesus of Galilee and the Historical Peasant," in *Archaeology and the Galilee: Texts and Contexts in the Graeco-Roman and Byzantine Periods* (eds. D. R. Edwards and C. T. McCollough; USF Studies in the History of Judaism 143; Atlanta: Scholars Press, 1997), 67–74.

29. David Aden-Bayewitz, *Common Pottery in Roman Galilee: A Study of Local Trade* (Ramat Gan: Bar-Ilan University Press, 1993).

Jewish Death Ritual
in Early Roman Palestine

The G. W. Thompson Chapel of Remembrance, a small funeral home in Spartanburg, S.C., recently added a new option to the array of services available to its clients in their time of sorrow. In addition to the customary preparations, visitation, and interment that have long been traditional in the American Southeast, Thompson Chapel has begun to offer a rather less conventional ritual as well—"drive-thru viewing." On the evening before the funeral, at the close of the visitation service, clients may choose to have the open casket rolled to a position in front of a lighted 4 ft. x 8 ft. plate-glass window looking out onto the parking lot. A sign on the wall outside invites drivers to turn into a lane leading up to the window, where they can view the body of the deceased from the comfort and privacy of their cars. Christine Thompson, vice president of Thompson Chapel, explains "drive-thru viewing" this way: "We try to make it convenient for our people in their time of hurting. Some people are too afraid to come inside to view the body. Others don't get off work until after hours, or they are disabled and find it difficult to get around."[1] In spite of these attractions, Ms. Thompson concedes that only about 30 percent of clients have opted to have their loved one displayed in the window. In addition, only one other funeral home in Spartanburg (a metropolitan region of nearly 100,000 inhabitants) took the step of adding a "drive-thru window" to their facilities, only to abandon it shortly thereafter. The National Funeral Directors and Morticians Association reports that "drive-thru viewing" is "not a common practice"[2] in American funeral homes.

But why not? Certainly the good people at Thompson Chapel were simply (in their own words) "trying to make it convenient"

for their clients during their time of need. Surely convenience
ought to have a powerful appeal to potential clients, especially in the
prosperous and increasingly competitive service economy of the
southeastern United States. Yet in this case it clearly does not.
Among the many reasons that may contribute to the relative unpop-
ularity of "drive-thru viewing" at Thompson Chapel, one of the most
significant is the role that death ritual plays in a society and culture.
Burial practices support a society's battle against death by celebrat-
ing symbolic representations of the society's most valorized patterns
for living. Ceremonial observances in death ritual are typically replete
with images of all that is believed to make life worth living. From
this perspective the reluctance of Thompson's clients to participate
in a "drive-by" death ritual is not only understandable, it might even
have been predictable. Convenience and comfort would have to lie
very close to the heart of southeastern American culture in order for
representations of those values to function with power in a funerary
ritual context. But ease and convenience do not in fact have deep
roots in the webs of signification and meaning by which the collective patterns of life in the social structure of Spartanburg, S.C. are
organized. On the contrary, social relations in that part of the United
States are still significantly shaped by traditional southern cultural
constructs of courtesy, consideration, civility, and kindness, values
that "drive-thru viewing" neither celebrates nor symbolically represents. Ease and convenience may be prominent factors in *economic*
decision making, but they are not among the norms and values upon
which social relations have traditionally been based. In developing
their "drive-thru" facility, then, Christine Thompson and her colleagues made the mistake of confusing consumer values, which drive
economic decision making, with the cultural values which organize
a social system and which death ritual exists to celebrate.

Death ritual, in other words, is cultural. It belongs to the web
of significations and meanings by which a society organizes the
pattern of its collective life, and it gives symbolic expression to
convictions and beliefs that are situated near the foundation of a
social system. Analyses of funerary practice that overlook the priority of culture are bound to fail.[3] This fact is particularly important
to the study of death ritual in early Roman Palestine (63 B.C.E.–135
C.E.), since in this region and period the history of Judaism and
Christianity unfolded within the context of a common culture

shared by both Jews and Christians. Events were moving rapidly in
Palestine during the early Roman period. Rome consolidated power
over the region and then suppressed with brutal efficiency not one
but two popular revolts. Herod the Great assisted the Romans in
establishing hegemony over Palestine and remained in power himself longer than any other client-king in the history of the Roman
Empire. His family dynasty reigned in whole or in part for three
generations. The temple in Jerusalem was built and destroyed.
Urbanization came to the Galilee as Herod Antipas built the city of
Tiberias and turned Sepphoris into the "ornament of all Galilee."
Jesus of Nazareth lived and died, and his followers emerged as a sect
within the common Judaism of the time. Another sect of Jews
stored their writings in jars and hid them in caves near the Dead
Sea. Early rabbis such as Hillel and Shammai laid the foundation for
the most influential body of Jewish legal literature since the Torah.
And along with all these famous and influential historical figures
and groups, there were also hundreds and thousands of ordinary
people who lived and died and were buried in a culture that was
gradually beginning to be reshaped and re-formed under the steady
pressure of Greek and Roman influences from the West. Clear signs
of the interplay of these influences are evident in the death ritual of
Roman Palestine. The rise of the Jewish ossuary is one example.
With these individual containers for secondary burial, longstanding
local burial customs were finding a new form of expression and
incorporating cultural values from another land. The rapidly spread-
ing popularity of the *loculus* niche also indicates the attraction that
Palestinian Jews could feel toward the cultural artifacts of Greece
and Rome. Even the Roman custom of putting a coin in the mouth
of the deceased eventually came to be practiced by a few Jewish
families in and around Jerusalem. During the early Roman period,
however, these Hellenistic influences were not yet as strong as they
would eventually come to be. During the first century, a strong and
vibrant Jewish culture in Palestine was able to incorporate these
newer influences without losing touch with its indigenous values
and rituals. For the vast majority of ordinary people, traditional customs and practices—including death ritual—continued to wield substantial symbolic power. In matters of death and burial, in other
words, Jews and Christians in early Roman Palestine shared a common Jewish ethnicity.

   The following discussion of Jewish burial practices in early
Roman Palestine will make selective use of some rabbinic sources,
and since current scholarly opinion is openly suspicious about the
use of such documents as a historical source for the early Roman
period, a brief word of explanation is necessary at this point. Of
course we can no longer assume, as an earlier generation of scholars
did, that the third-century Mishnah necessarily preserves reliable
information about first-century Jewish life. In many cases it
demonstrably does not. On the specific topic of death ritual, however, there are good reasons to think that careful use of the
Mishnah—in conjunction with other evidence—can make a contribution to a historical reconstruction of the early Roman period.
Those reasons arise from both archaeology and anthropology. At
points where it can be checked against the archaeological evidence,
the Mishnah has already been shown to provide a representative
reflection of some aspects of burial practices from the early Roman
period. *M. B. Bat.* 6:8, for example, records a discussion among
Tannaitic rabbis about the ideal dimensions for burial niches. The
figures discussed by R. Simeon and R. Simeon b. Gamaliel correspond quite closely to the actual size of early Roman burial caves
and *loculus* niches. In *m. B. Bat.* 2:9, Rabbi Akiba declares that
tombs should be located at least fifty cubits outside the limits of
habitation in a city or town. Archaeology confirms that tombs
were indeed located at least that far from settlements across early
Roman Palestine, including Jerusalem, Qumran, and Khirbet Cana.
Akiba is said to have taught that tombs should not be located to the
west of a town or city (presumably because the prevailing wind
usually comes from that direction), and this too was the practice at
many early Roman sites. It is not necessary to suppose, and we
should not imagine, that ordinary people consciously "obeyed" the
specific dictates of rabbinic teachings. The important point here is
only that *when it comes to the specific topic of death ritual,* the rabbinic
sources—even though they are later than the early Roman
period—have been shown to record information that generally
conforms with the patterns evident in the material remains of early
Roman Jewish burial customs. In addition, it is something of an
anthropological commonplace that burial practices typically
change only in response to significant alterations in the social
structure. Theological ideas about death and the afterlife often are

quite vague and fluid, but the public ritual process of death has a weight and mass all its own. From this perspective it would not be especially remarkable if a third-century document were to preserve useful information about burial customs from two centuries earlier. For all these reasons, this discussion does not hesitate to make critical use of texts from the Mishnah, along with the talmudic tractate *Semahot*—always in conjunction with other sources of evidence— in order to reconstruct a composite picture of typical Jewish burial practices in early Roman Palestine. The following portrait of those practices, in other words, is based on the combined testimony of texts and tombs.

Jewish funerals in this region and period, whether in Judea or the Galilee, generally took place as soon as possible after death, most often before sunset on the same day. In two early Christian stories, both of which originated in early Roman Palestine, burial takes place just that promptly. Funeral preparations for Jairus's daughter begin within a few hours of her death (Mark 5:38), and in John 11 Lazarus too is buried on the same day as his death. Rabbinic sources paint a similar picture. *M. Sanh.* 6:5 expresses the preference that a corpse should be kept unburied overnight only if the extra time is needed to prepare a bier and/or the grave wrappings.

Semahot 1:4–5 also presumes that burial will be prompt when it argues that no preparations should begin before it is certain that death has occurred, and *Sem.* 9:9 contends that burial should be "hastened" whenever possible. The only exception is the burial of one's parents, in which case the bereaved should "make an elaborate funeral and not hasten the burial." The preference for prompt burial was so strong, in fact, that in some cases bodies apparently were interred a little too quickly. *Sem.* 8.1 relates the story of two people who were discovered to have been buried alive: "A man was inspected after three days, and he went on to live twenty-five years; still another went on to have five children and died later."

Preparations typically began as soon as death was certain: the eyes were closed, and the corpse was washed, and then wrapped and bound. Literary depictions often suggest that perfumes or ointments were used for this washing. The terminology of "wrapping and binding," found in numerous rabbinic texts, describes a process in which the jaw was closed, the hands fixed along the sides of the body, and the feet tied together at the ankles (*Sem.* 1:2–5,

12:10). The Lazarus narrative has preparations of this sort in view when it says that Lazarus's "hands and feet were bound with strips of cloth, and his face was wrapped in a cloth" (John 11:44). Some rabbinic texts argue that the task of "wrapping and binding" must be gender specific: men, the rabbis suggest, may wrap and bind the corpse of a man, but not that of a woman. Women, by contrast, may wrap and bind either a male or a female corpse. Thus "wrapped and bound," the corpse was carried out in a procession toward the place of interment, accompanied by friends, neighbors, and relatives. Such processions are described in the New Testament (e.g., Luke 7:12) and in Josephus, who emphasizes the splendor of Herod's funerary cortege (*Jewish War* 1.671–3). On a more humble scale, the rabbis considered what should be done if a funeral procession were to encounter a wedding procession. The funeral, they said, ought to yield the right of way: "The deceased must make way for the bride, the honor of the living coming before the honor of the dead" (*Sem.* 11:6). There were other reasons for stopping the procession as well: several Mishnaic texts suggest that processions occasionally halted in order to "make lamentation" for the dead (e.g., *m. Meg.* 4:3; *m. B. Bat.* 6:7). Unfortunately, the texts do not clarify the specific contours of the practice, and since neither narrative descriptions nor material remains survive, it is impossible for us to know precisely what sort of ritual activities might have been involved.

Jewish funeral processions made their way from the *home* of the family of the deceased to the *tomb* of the family of the deceased. These tombs were customarily located outside the limits of human habitation in villages, towns, and cities, and were carved into the soft limestone bedrock that is so common in the geology of Syro-Palestine. Literary depictions of tombs and burial places often explicitly describe rock-cut caves with stone-covered entrances (e.g., John 11:38; Mark 15:46), and the archaeological remains are plentiful. So many tombs have been excavated and published, in fact, that not only can typical features and characteristics be identified, but changes in those characteristics over time can also be observed.[4] The burial caves excavated by Vasilios Tzaferis in 1968 at Giv'at ha-Mivtar are still broadly representative of the typical pattern for Jewish tombs from the early Roman period, and Tomb 1 at Giv'at ha-Mivtar can serve to illustrate many of their characteristic features.[5] Entry into this two-chambered tomb began with an external forecourt, one wall of which contained a small entryway, approximately .5 m x .5 m x .8 m, leading into the first of two burial chambers. The outer face of the entryway, which bore no ornamentation or decoration, was covered by a stone that had been worked to fit snugly into the opening. Small, narrow entrances of this sort, covered by stones, are the typical path of entry into most Jewish tombs in early Roman Palestine. In many cases—including, for example, Tomb 4 at Giv'at ha-Mivtar—the stone was worked and shaped into a recessed design so that it fit tightly into the entryway, while its outer face had a wider flange that completely covered the edges of the entryway. The typical stone that covered the entrance to a Jewish tomb in early Roman Palestine was thus nearly square or slightly rectangular in shape. It is actually quite rare for these stones to be round, or to be situated in such a way as to be rolled away from the entrance to the tomb. Examples of round and/or rolling stones are not unknown— the Tombs of the Kings and "Herod's" tomb in Jerusalem, for example—but they appear to have been limited to relatively few tombs belonging to the very wealthy in and around Jerusalem. In most cases the stone would have had to be pulled or dragged, not rolled, from the entrance.

The narrow doorway to Tomb 1 at Giv'at ha-Mivtar leads into the first of two burial chambers within the tomb itself. Each chamber is roughly equal in size, measuring approximately three meters in length and width, with a height of about one meter. In the center of each chamber a depression had been carved into the floor to a depth of one-half meter, most likely to facilitate the process of moving about and working within the tomb. This depression— Tzaferis calls it a "central pit,"[6] while others use the term "standing pit"—created a low shelf running around three sides of the chamber. Above the shelf, a total of twelve *loculus* niches had been carved into the walls of the chambers, four in chamber A and eight in chamber B.[7] Five of the niches were open, but seven of them were sealed, either by a flat slab of stone or by a pile of small stones.

The use of underground chambers for burial had a long background in the region of Syro-Palestine, going back at least as far as the Chalcolithic Age, when the dead first began to be laid to rest by family groups in small rock-cut caves.[8] Over time the simple, round chambers of the Chalcolithic and Bronze Ages evolved into the more sophisticated architecture of the Iron Age "bench" tomb. In these tombs, a bench or shelf—approximately waist-high—ran along three sides of the roughly square burial chamber. The central depression in early Roman tombs like Tomb 1 at Giv'at ha-Mivtar may be a vestigial remnant of this "bench" tomb architecture from the Iron Age. The *loculus* niche was a more recent addition to the architecture of Jewish burial caves. These deep narrow niches—typically .5 m x .6 m x 1.5-2.0 m—originated in the Hellenistic world and first entered the land of Palestine at Maresha during the third century B.C.E.[9] They quickly became very popular, and by the middle of the first century C.E. they were the most widely used form of burial niche in Palestine. The architectural features of Tomb 1 at Giv'at ha-Mivtar thus highlight both the tradition and the innovation that characterized Jewish burial practices in early Roman Palestine.

An additional innovation, although one that did not appear in the Giv'at ha-Mivtar tombs, was the *arcosolium* burial niche. Unlike a *loculus*, which is a deep narrow slot carved into the wall of a tomb, an *arcosolium* niche is a broad arch-shaped recess carved along the wall of a tomb, creating a wide and open shelf upon which a body could be laid. While a corpse placed in a *loculus* niche would lie perpendicular to the wall of the tomb, so that at most only the feet or head would be visible, a corpse laid in an *arcosolium* niche would lie parallel to the wall of the tomb. The entire body of the deceased would be in view, lying on a shelf beneath an arch-shaped recess. Typically 1.5–2.0 meters wide, with an arch 1.0–1.5 meters high, an *arcosolium* thus occupies considerably more wall space than a *loculus*, and a burial chamber with *arcosolia* will naturally contain fewer niches than a *loculus* cave. Like the *loculus* niche, however, the *arcosolium* was also a Hellenistic development that first began to appear in Jewish tombs in Palestine during the late Hellenistic and Herodian periods. Examples are known from (among others) the "Tombs of the Kings" in Jerusalem, Dominus Flevit, Akeldama, and Beth She'arim.[10]

The quality of workmanship in the construction of Jewish tombs in early Roman Palestine can vary dramatically. A few tombs— in particular, some large, multi-chambered caves from Jerusalem— are characterized by precise dimensions, squared corners, finished surfaces, and decorative friezes and carvings. In one chamber in the tombs at Akeldama, for instance, panels in sunken relief ornamented the walls beneath neatly worked *arcosolium* niches, and in the corners were carved representations of Doric columns. The entryway to another chamber was laid out in *distyle in antis* ("two-columned porch") format, and the burial chamber itself featured a smooth domed ceiling. Other well-constructed tombs from early Roman Jerusalem include the "Tombs of the Kings" and the Sanedria tombs. Certainly the families who owned and used these caves must have been situated among the higher socioeconomic classes, for the creation of funerary architecture of this sort must have involved substantial resources. Most Jewish burial caves in this region and period, however, are not luxurious at all, but roughly hewn, with irregular dimensions, unfinished surfaces, and an absence of decoration. It is not unusual, for example, for *loculus* niches to be so unevenly arranged—and cut into the wall at such odd angles—that one niche actually runs into another. A poorly constructed tomb might appear to be evidence of a family's lower social and economic status, but conclusions of this sort require careful review, since rich families may have had the means to build a splendid tomb but simply chose to use their wealth in other ways. In fact there would have been little social incentive for Jewish families in this region and period to expend resources on the construction and ornamentation of a tomb's interior. During the typical Jewish funeral, after all, the inside of the tomb would have been visible to few if any of the spectators. Members of the immediate family usually placed the body in the tomb while friends and relatives waited outside. A roughly hewn burial chamber might therefore be evidence not of a family's poverty, but rather of their inclination to spend wealth in other ways. Indeed in one case—the famous "Caiaphas" tomb from south of Jerusalem—the construction of the tomb's interior was uneven and unfinished, with rounded corners on two sides and walls of erratic proportions. Clearly this family was not inclined to spend money on the construction of their tomb's interior. Yet the ossuary that was found in this tomb inscribed with the name "Caiaphas" is among the most beautiful specimens in the archaeological record, with elaborate rosettes on its outer face framed by branches sprouting upward to both sides of the rosettes. The lid, which was vaulted, had been painted orange.[11] The family of "Caiaphas," in other words, spent their wealth on some aspects of funerary practice but not others. Simple and straightforward deductions about wealth and class based solely upon the quality of funerary artifacts must therefore be resisted.

The skeletal remains in the burial chambers of Tomb 1 at Giv'at ha-Mivtar illustrate the general pattern of burial practices that was customary for Jewish family groups in early Roman Palestine. Two forms of interment are common: (1) primary burial, in which the body of the deceased was placed in the tomb at the time of death; and (2) secondary burial, in which the bones of the deceased were gathered after the flesh of the corpse had decomposed. Both primary and secondary burial were widely practiced by Jewish families in early Roman Palestine, and both were present at Giv'at ha-Mivtar. A single skeleton, for example, was found in each of the *loculus* niches in the tomb. The bodies lay lengthwise in the niches, most of them head first, so that the feet of each corpse lay closest to the open end of the niche. Primary burial in niches—both *loculi* and *arcosolia*—is common in the Jewish tombs of early Roman Palestine, with parallel examples elsewhere in Jerusalem, Jericho, and in the Galilee at Huqoq, to name a few. Niches were not, however, the only location in a tomb wherein the remains of the deceased might be laid at the time of primary burial. In many tombs skeletal remains have also been found on the low shelf around the standing pit, indicating that bodies were laid on this shelf at the time of primary burial. Less frequent—and not represented at Giv'at ha-Mivtar—were primary burials in free-standing burial containers, such as sarcophagi or coffins. Sarcophagi, that is, stone containers used for the primary burial of one body, are often richly ornamented and tend to be found more often in the tombs of the wealthy. The sarcophagus of Queen Helene of Adiabene, from the "Tombs of the Kings," is a good example, as are the sarcophagi from several sites described by R. H. Smith.[12] All of these sarcophagi featured characteristic similarities in size, workmanship, and decoration, including geometric and floral friezes carved into raised panels on their anterior faces. Coffins, like sarcophagi, are freestanding and movable containers used for the burial of one body, but are made from lead or wood rather than stone. Wooden coffins are often evident only in the metal nails and hinges they leave behind, but Rachel Hachlili and Ann Killebrew have now reported on well-preserved wooden coffins, artfully constructed and ornamented, in the early Roman Jewish necropolis at Jericho.[13]

Upon arriving at the tomb, then, participants in a Jewish funeral procession in early Roman Palestine stood by while members of the immediate family placed the body of their deceased loved one in the tomb. Textual sources variously describe the rituals that unfolded at this point, but none (unfortunately) describes the process in full detail. Eulogies were spoken, and personal effects of the deceased might be placed in the tomb alongside the body (*Sem.* 8:2–7). An inkwell, for example, was said to have been buried along with Samuel the Small (*Sem.* 8:7), and the discovery of an inkwell in a tomb at Meiron has provided material confirmation.[14] Other personal items that appear include jewelry, combs, and sandals. Ehud Netzer has reported on a Jewish tomb from the early Roman period in Jericho that included a "mourning enclosure" around the entrance to the tomb, and it is likely that this space was the setting for public lamentation and eulogizing of the deceased.[15] Included in this enclosure were rows of bench seats located in the area above the entrance to the tomb, so that members of the procession could seat themselves on these benches for the eulogies and deposition. Similar benches are known from the catacombs at Beth She'arim. Some literary sources describe a ceremony in which friends and neighbors arranged themselves in rows in order to offer condolences to the bereaved, in a kind of receiving line (*m. Ber.* 3:2; *m. Meg.* 4:3; *m. Sanh.* 2:1; *Sem.* 10:9). Here too the details of the ritual are not clear: some texts suggest that the row of friends and neighbors stood still as the mourners passed by, while others indicate that the mourners stood still as a row of friends and neighbors passed by. No doubt there were local variations, but it is clear that the ceremony of primary burial customarily included a public delivery of eulogies as well as ritual demonstration of sympathy for the bereaved. Expressions of condolence could be offered both at the tomb and at the home of the deceased after the procession had returned there.

The rituals of death did not come to end, however, with the funeral procession and the ceremony of primary burial. On the contrary, the public ritual process continued for some time thereafter. Members of the immediate family participated in rites of

mourning that unfolded over the following weeks and months.
Literary sources agree that for the first seven days after the death,
members of the immediate family customarily remained at home,
mourning for the deceased. During this seven-day period, which the
rabbis appropriately called *shiv'ah* (seven), mourners were expected
to abstain from working, bathing, wearing shoes, and most forms of
social participation (*Sem.* 6:1). Several rabbinic sources speak of
"inverting the bed" during these days of mourning, probably a
euphemism for abstinence from sexual activity. The literary sources
presume that if mourners leave the house during this time, they do
so in order to visit the tomb. The Lazarus narrative, for example,
relates that when Lazarus's sister Mary leaves the family home,
neighbors and friends go along with her, "assuming that she was
going to the tomb in order to grieve there" (John. 11:31). Rabbinic
sources presume that this period of mourning lasts for seven days,
and some later texts record careful deliberations among the rabbis
regarding the proper enumeration of those days (*Sem.* 7:1–7).

The seven days of *shiv'ah* were followed, the rabbis maintained,
by thirty more days of mourning, which they designated (again,
appropriately) by the Hebrew term *shloshim* (thirty). During this
period the bereaved slowly began the process of re-entering the
normal flow of social interaction. They were no longer expected,
for example, to remain at home. Some rabbinic texts indicate that
the bereaved still did not work (*Sem.* 9:14) or participate in social
gatherings or festive occasions (*Sem.* 9:15), but a gradual process of
normalization was certainly underway. As *Sem.* 10:12 describes it:
"On the first sabbath (after the death), the mourner should not
enter the synagogue. On the second, he may enter, but may not sit
in his place. On the third, he may enter and sit in his place, but may
not speak. On the fourth, he is like everyone else."

By the end of the *shloshim*, in other words, the separation of the
mourner from full participation in society was largely ended. In
the terminology of Arnold van Gennep's *The Rites of Passage*, the
completion of *shloshim* marked the point at which the mourner was
reincorporated (or reintegrated) into the social system. As the rabbis put it, "he is like everyone else." Rituals of mourning extended
beyond the thirty days of *shloshim* only in the case of the death of
one's parent(s). Children were expected to continue mourning for
their parents until a full year had passed.

The ritual process of burial came to its completion after a year had passed, with the ceremony of secondary burial, when the bones of the deceased were gathered after the flesh of the body had decomposed. The tombs at Giv'at ha-Mivtar, like most Jewish tombs from early Roman Palestine, featured more than one form of secondary burial. Eight ossuaries, for example, were found in various locations around Tomb 1—three of them together in one *loculus*—and each contained the bones of at least one person. One of the ossuaries (4) was inscribed with the name Yehohanan and contained the bones of an adult male who had been crucified, along with the bones of a child. In addition, a small pit (approximately 1 m x 1 m x .3 m) had also been dug into the floor on the west side of chamber B, and this pit was found to contain the reburied bones of a child. In this way Tomb 1 typifies a pattern that is evident throughout the archaeological record of Jewish burial in early Roman Palestine: secondary burial is the dominant practice, but it appears in a variety of forms. Ossuaries are common in and around Jerusalem from the late first century B.C.E. until the early second century C.E., basically from Herod until Bar Kokhba. In the Galilee, by contrast, ossuaries are (thus far) unknown before the second century C.E., when they first appear in a cluster of Jewish tombs at Huqoq. Other forms of secondary burial are more typical, including secondary burial in pits, niches, and even on the shelf or floor of the tomb chamber. In a first-century C.E. tomb from French Hill, a case of secondary burial was found in which the bones had been reburied in one corner of the central depression of the tomb chamber, with "four long bones radiating from the northeast corner, surmounted by a skull."[16] Thus while secondary burial was the prevalent pattern for Jewish burial in early Roman Palestine, there was considerable variety in its practice. Within the privacy of the family tomb, everyone did what was right in their own eyes.

The concentration of Jewish ossuaries in and around early Roman Jerusalem is, however, important to the social history of this region and period. The reasons for the concentration of ossuaries in the area around Jerusalem have long been puzzling to archaeologists and historians.[17] Completely unknown before 30 B.C.E., they proliferated rapidly during the first century C.E. Eric M. Meyers argued that parallels to the Jewish ossuary can be found in similar types of ancient Near Eastern containers for secondary burial.[18] Drawing upon examples from as far away as Persia and Crete, he regarded the ossuary as a Jewish adaptation of a widespread ancient Near Eastern funerary practice. Levi Rahmani vehemently disagreed, describing the ossuary instead as a distinctively "Jerusalemite" artifact that evolved locally and independently of any outside influence.[19] More recently the ossuary has increasingly come to be regarded as the result of a constellation of both local and nonlocal factors, especially as it arose within the context of the encounter between Judaism and Hellenism. In Jerusalem during the first century C.E., traditional Jewish customs of secondary burial were intersecting with newer Hellenistic constructs of the human individual. The increasing influence of Hellenism—particularly Hellenistic cultural norms valorizing the human individual—provides the most plausible and proximate cause for the emergence of a form of secondary burial that preserved individual identity. The ossuary is best understood, in other words, as an artifact of the intersection between Judaism and Hellenism, and as such it exemplifies what Meyers has called Hellenism's ability to "serve as a framework for preserving and promoting local Semitic culture."[20]

A Jewish ossuary from the early Roman period is a chest or box, usually made of stone but occasionally of clay or wood, used for secondary burial. Hollowed out from blocks of the soft limestone that is so common in Syro-Palestine, ossuaries are typically proportionate in size to the large and long bones of the body (e.g., skull and femur). Thus the average size of an adult's ossuary is approximately 60 cm x 35 cm x 30 cm, with smaller measurements for children. In keeping with their function, ossuaries have removable lids, most of which are flat, although some are domed or gabled. The majority of ossuaries are plain and undecorated, but many are ornamented with decorations typical of artistic motifs in the early Roman Jewish art.[21] Geometric designs, for example, appear very frequently, the most common of which is a six-petalled rosette, which was chip-carved into the side of the ossuary using a chisel and compass.[22] Representations of Jewish religious themes also appear, including palm branches, menorahs, and Torah shrines. Inscriptions, when present, are scrawled with charcoal or scratched with a nail or sharp object, and may be found virtually anywhere on the ossuary, including the sides, ends, lid, or even along the inside edge. These inscriptions typically include only the name of the deceased, and sometimes a nickname, patronymic, or place of origin. Occasionally a distinguishing fact about the deceased may also be added. In view of the fact that ossuaries emerged during the engagement of Judaism with Hellenism, it is significant that slightly more than 40 percent of inscriptions on Jewish ossuaries from the early Roman period are in Greek.[23]

Ossuaries are found in Jewish tombs from early Roman Palestine, most often in tombs within the vicinity of Jerusalem.[24] In this regard Tomb 1 at Giv'at ha-Mivtar is typical. Secondary burial in ossuaries took place at the end of a long process of burial and mourning, when decomposition of the flesh was complete—or nearly so. Some rabbinic texts actually caution against gathering bones too soon. *Semahot* 12:6, for example, argues that "the bones of a corpse should not be taken apart, nor the tendons severed, unless the bones had fallen apart of themselves and the tendons of themselves had been severed," and Rabbi Akiba is reported to have taught that "the bones may not be gathered until the flesh has wasted away; once it has, the features are no longer recognizable in the skeleton" (*Sem.* 12:7). In a private ceremony which was attended only by family members, and which took place entirely within the confines of the family burial cave, the bones of the deceased were taken from their resting place on the shelf or in a niche and collected in an ossuary. The ossuary might then be marked with the name of the deceased and positioned in its final resting place—either on the floor, on the shelf, or in a niche. When ossuaries were placed in *loculi*, the openings of the niches were often sealed over with stone slabs. *Semahot* 12.9, for example, describes the rite of secondary burial rather poignantly:

> Rabbi Eleazar bar Zadok said: "Thus spoke my father at the time of his death: 'My son, bury me first in a niche. In the course of time, collect my bones and put them in an ossuary; but do not gather them with your own hands.' And thus did I attend him: Johanan entered, collected the bones, and spread a sheet over them. I then came in, rent my clothes for them, and sprinkled dried herbs over them. Just as he attended his father, so I attended him." (*Sem.* 12:9)

Other sources (e.g., Q 9:59–60) also emphasize the connection between secondary burial and the family group.

Individual secondary burial of this sort had virtually no history in Jerusalem, or anywhere else in Syro-Palestine, prior to the early Roman period. On the contrary, for centuries the dominant pattern throughout the region had been *collective* secondary burial, in which the bones of the deceased were piled together in a common heap along with the bones of all previously deceased family members. As far back as the late Bronze Age, for example, bones were gathered together on one side of a roughly circular underground tomb. By the Iron Age II, this simple late Bronze Age tomb architecture had evolved into the Israelite "bench tomb," in which a low bench ran along three sides of a roughly square cave. At the time of primary burial, bodies were laid on the shelf to decompose, and when decomposition was complete, the bones were gathered into a recess hollowed out beneath the bench. Over time these recesses came to hold the bones of all family members long dead, so that the material culture of Iron Age secondary burial is vividly captured in the familiar biblical expression, "he slept and was gathered to his fathers."[25] Collective secondary burial of this sort persisted into the closing decades of the first century B.C.E., when charnel rooms were common in many Jewish tombs of the late Hellenistic and early Roman periods. In these tombs, bones of family members were piled together in a separate chamber prepared and reserved exclusively for that purpose.[26] At the conclusion of this kind of collective secondary burial, the remains of the deceased would have been rendered completely indistinguishable from the remains of the "fathers." The identity of the individual would have been thoroughly dissolved into an ancestral collective. In the common heap of bones beneath the bench of an Iron Age II tomb or in the charnel room of a late Hellenistic tomb, it would have been completely impossible for surviving relatives to identify the remains of any individual deceased family member. With the ossuary, by contrast, the identity of the deceased was preserved even after death and secondary burial because the individual container—often marked with the name of the deceased—conserved and protected his or her individuality.[27]

Several attempts to account for the rise of the Jewish ossuary have been unsatisfactory because they have sought to explain the ossuary primarily as an expression of Jewish theological convictions and religious beliefs. A particularly common view has held that the ossuary arose from Jewish convictions about death and the afterlife, especially belief in the bodily resurrection of the dead.[28] Drawing upon late rabbinic sources, including some that suggest that decomposition of the flesh could expiate sin (*b. Sabb.* 13b; *b. Qidd. 31b; b. Sanh. 47b; b. Ber.* 18b), this view has maintained that individual secondary burial in ossuaries served as a ritual preparation of the dead for the day of resurrection. Gathering the bones of the deceased in an ossuary supposedly gave symbolic representation to the fact that the deceased was purified from sin and ready to be raised. The rise of the ossuary, in other words, was driven by the rise of belief in bodily resurrection. The weakness of this argument is obvious and does not need to be belabored here. Suffice it to say that no sources from the early Roman period associate the ossuary with belief in the resurrection, and talmudic sources are simply too late to be used as uncorroborated evidence for Jewish religious beliefs in the first century C.E.

It is unfortunate that academic discussion of the Jewish ossuary has not made use of an insight that has become a commonplace in the anthropology of death ritual, namely, that death ritual is intimately related to social structure. Ever since the early twentieth century, when Robert Hertz first traced the extent of social determination in funerary practice, it has become increasingly clear that ritual disposal of the dead is laden with symbolic representations and ceremonial performances that express, celebrate, reinforce, and repair a social system.[29] The performance of death ritual is driven not primarily by the psychological needs of individuals, nor even by the religious convictions of groups, but by tasks and conflicts that confront society as a whole. For death is more than just the ending of the physical life of a mortal body: it is also a hole in the fabric of a society, a void where once there were bonds that tied people together. Death forcibly removes a member of a social network, and in so doing, calls into question the ongoing viability of the network as a whole. Death ritual, Hertz argued, is a social process that meets the threat of death head on. Social structure is established through death ritual, in other words, and changes in death ritual, when they occur, usually are associated with developments in social structure. As Ian Morris has succinctly put it, "In ritual people use symbols to make social structure explicit."[30] A compelling account of the rise of the Jewish ossuary, then, should connect the emergence of these bone containers with changes in the social structure of Jerusalem during the late first century B.C.E. and the early first century C.E.

Steven Fine has recently taken a step in this direction by proposing that the rise of the ossuary reflects "a general pattern of individuation within the Greco-Roman world."[31] Citing both economic and cultural factors, he argues that the prosperity of Jerusalem under Herod the Great, along with "developing notions of the individual's place within the family unit,"[32] provided the means and the motive for Jews in Jerusalem to begin practicing a form of secondary burial that preserved individual identity. "Clearly there were Jews in first-century Jerusalem for whom the identity of each individual was important."[33] This is the beginning of a good argument. Certainly the building programs of Herod the Great did bring economic prosperity in general, and a thriving stone-carving industry in particular, to Jerusalem. Some ossuaries, such as the "Caiaphas" ossuary with its richly ornamented rosettes, or some of the specimens from the Akeldama tombs, betray an unmistakable level of affluence. Be that as it may, economic prosperity still does not account for the rise of the Jewish ossuary. For although some are ornately decorated and elegantly crafted, many (if not most) ossuaries are of quite crude construction—roughly hewn, unevenly formed, and lacking any kind of decoration. Such artifacts are certainly not the products of skilled workmanship nor are they monuments of material affluence. In addition, while economic prosperity may be able to explain the rising quality of some funerary artifacts in early Roman Jerusalem, it does not account for the change in the form of burial ritual during this time. For rising standards of living in and of themselves do not demand a shift from *collective* secondary burial in charnel rooms to *individual* secondary burial in ossuaries. Prosperous Jews in first-century Jerusalem could equally well have hired skilled stone-carvers to construct elaborately ornamented charnel rooms for their family tombs. Of course they did not—they began to use ossuaries instead. Economic developments in first-century Jerusalem do not, then, provide a sufficient background for the rise of the Jewish ossuary. A more likely source for the social energy that produced the ossuary would be a change of some sort in the role of the individual in family and society in early Roman Jerusalem.

Certainly Jewish society in Jerusalem had undergone profound changes in the centuries immediately prior to the early Roman period, and during this time no influence was more substantial or long-lasting than the culture of Hellenism. Even before Alexander the Great had conquered the eastern end of the Mediterranean, traders and mercenaries from the Aegean had already made their way to Palestine, bringing with them the Attic coins and black-figured wares that regularly surface in Persian period strata of archaeological excavations. As early as the middle of the fifth century B.C.E., "the handwriting was already on the wall, and it was in Greek."[34] Later, under the auspices of Roman political and military authority, the cultural streams of Judaism and Hellenism came to terms with each other more fully, and in specific and creative ways. All Jews in Palestine (indeed, all Jews in the ancient world) became "hellenized" to one degree or another, as every area of life—language, politics, education, architecture, literature, religion, and material culture—absorbed a cultural imprint whose origins were in Greece. While the depth of this imprint varied from place to place, by the early Roman period its breadth covered most of Syro-Palestine. Death ritual was among the areas of culture that Hellenism had touched. Even before the early Roman period the process of hellenization had already begun to introduce recognizable changes into Jewish death ritual in Palestine. Primary burial in sarcophagi, for example, increased during the early Hellenistic period, and the *loculus* niche—a Hellenistic form of tomb architecture—also came into Palestine during the first century B.C.E.[35] Even the Greco-Roman custom of putting a coin in the mouth of the deceased (to pay Charon, the ferryman across the river Styx) eventually came to be practiced by some Jewish families, including the family of Caiaphas the high priest. All of these burial customs are of Hellenistic origin, so the ossuary would certainly not have been the first aspect of Jewish death ritual to be touched by the interaction of Judaism with Hellenism. In addition, these changes in Jewish death ritual valorize the human individual in ways that had been consistently celebrated in Hellenism. Greek politics had long valued the voice of the individual in the democratic process, and Greek theater was steeped in the tradition of tragedians like

Sophocles, who had dramatized the psychological strengths and weaknesses of individual human beings. Greek sculptors of the Hellenistic period had pursued an artistic quest for the ideal human form, and Greek educators took up that quest on an individual level through the physical exercises that were a staple of training in the *gymnasium*.

The emergence of Hellenistic burial practices in Palestine suggests that by the late first century B.C.E. the structure of Jewish society in and around Jerusalem was beginning to make more room for the human individual. Shaye Cohen has aptly described the development of post-biblical Judaism as the "democratization" of traditional Israelite religion. He points out that while the piety of pre-exilic Israel centered on the group, "the piety of second temple Judaism centered on both the group and the individual."[36] This observation aptly fits the developments we are following here. The rise of the Jewish ossuary indicates that in the early Roman period, democratization was beginning to reach into the internal structure of Jewish families in Jerusalem, as individual secondary burial began to represent and celebrate individual identity and dignity, even after death and burial. In the privacy of the family tomb, usually with only one or two close relatives present, the social structure of the family was established in a way that protected and defended the individual. The persona of the deceased did not dissolve into an ancestral collective but was symbolically preserved for all time. Those who could afford it supplemented this symbolic preservation through ornamentation and decoration, and those who were literate inscribed it with a name, patronymic, or other epithet, but even the use of a roughly hewn, undecorated, and uninscribed ossuary still served to affirm the lasting value and eternal destiny of a discrete human being.

Glen Bowersock has written that in the ancient Mediterranean world, hellenization did not so much extinguish or overwhelm local customs as it provided fresh energy for their expression in new and innovative ways.[37] From this perspective the rise of the Jewish ossuary in early Roman Jerusalem is an exemplary case study in the power of Hellenism to influence a local culture, and in the resilience and creativity of a local culture in resisting it. By continuing to gather the bones of their dead, Jewish families in early Roman Jerusalem honored some of their most deeply rooted ancestral traditions, and by gathering bones in individual containers, those same families also embraced an emerging new pattern in their social system. This analysis may be able to account for what may be the most puzzling fact about the rise of the Jewish ossuary: Why Jerusalem? Why is the archaeological record for these bone containers so strongly concentrated around Jerusalem in the first century C.E.? If ossuaries are an artifact of the intersection between Judaism and Hellenism, then their appearance and concentration at Jerusalem (rather than somewhere else) is understandable. For only in the city of Jerusalem were traditional Jewish cultural norms and newer Hellenistic values both of sufficient strength to create the social energy that would be necessary to produce the ossuary. Only in Jerusalem were both Hellenism and Judaism sufficiently powerful cultural forces as to produce the kind of change in the social structure that would effect this synthesis. As an artifact of the intersection between Judaism and Hellenism, ossuaries arose in the one location where both of those cultural traditions were present in significant strength. Ossuaries did not arise at Caesarea Maritima, for example, because in that city the current of Hellenism was far stronger than Judaism, the city having been built from the ground up according to Greek and Roman norms. Nor did ossuaries arise in first-century Galilee, because there the opposite condition prevailed. In first-century Jerusalem, by contrast, Jewish and Hellenistic cultural constructs—traditions of secondary burial on the one hand and individual identity on the other—were intersecting with the dynamism it would take to produce an individual container for secondary burial.

In addition to ossuaries, the range of other artifacts typically found in Jewish tombs from early Roman Palestine can also help to illumine the contours of the social structure in this region and period. Lamps, perfume bottles, cooking pots, and the occasional coin all help to fill out our picture of life and death in that time and place. Lamps, for example, usually appear in the form of the "Herodian" lamp with its characteristic spatulate nozzle. Their presence in tomb chambers is largely self-explanatory, as the chambers were quite dark and family members would have needed at least some light in order to work and move around inside the tomb. Lamps would have been a functional necessity both at the time of primary burial and at the time of secondary burial. In keeping with this functional purpose, lamps are almost always found on the shelf around the central depression, and often near the entrance. It is rare to find a lamp inside a burial niche. Perfume bottles (*unguentaria*) also appear frequently, in both fusiform (spindle-bottle) and piriform (flat-bottomed with thin neck and bulbous body) shapes, each with a long narrow neck that would have helped to preserve and concentrate the scent of the perfume. Small globular juglets for perfumes are also common. Since corpses were washed with ointments in preparation for primary burial, these perfume bottles and juglets may have been used for that purpose. But washing and anointing the body appears to have customarily taken place at the home of the deceased prior to the funeral procession, not in the tomb chamber at the time of deposition. Indeed, family members would certainly have preferred to wash and anoint the body at home, rather than in the dark, cramped, and malodorous confines of the burial chamber itself. There are a few cases in which bones were anointed with oil or perfume at the time of secondary burial—as for example in some of the ossuaries from Tomb 1 at Giv'at ha-Mivtar—but the evidence for such practices is not widespread. A more plausible explanation for the presence of perfume bottles, then, has to do not with the bodies of the dead, but with the noses of the living. The smell inside a typical Jewish family burial cave of this region and period—with one or more bodies in various states of decomposition, awaiting secondary burial—must have been pungent indeed. Family members who entered the tomb would have needed not only a lamp to light the darkness but also an *unguentarium* to ward off the smell. The time they spent in the tomb would have been punctuated with short breaks during which they could relieve their senses by placing a perfume bottle under their noses. In keeping with this functional purpose, perfume bottles, like lamps, are typically found on the shelf around the standing pit, or on the floor of the standing pit. Jews in this region and period left large numbers of lamps and perfume bottles in their tombs, even though these articles would have continued to have value and utility in other contexts as well, especially in and around the home. Yet despite this potential usefulness, family members brought these vessels into their tombs and abandoned them there. The fact that they discarded perfectly good lamps and *unguentaria* in their tombs may be related to traditional Jewish constructs of corpse impurity. It may have been because they believed that such vessels, having come in contact with the dead, had contracted ritual impurity, that the Jews of early Roman Palestine left these vessels in their tombs. Of course the frequency of these functional vessels in Jewish tombs does not *prove* that they were abandoned for reasons of corpse impurity; it is simply consistent with that cultural norm.

In view of the conditions inside a typical Jewish family burial cave in early Roman Palestine—darkness, confinement, and stench—it is a curious fact that cooking pots are so often found therein. The ritual process of primary and secondary burial does not call for a cooking pot. Yet they appear in a broad majority of Jewish burial caves from this region and period, including both Judea and the Galilee, with representative examples at (to name a few) Giv'at ha-Mivtar, Jason's Tomb, French Hill, the "Caiaphas" tomb, Sanedria, Mahanayim, Rehov Nisan-Beq, Rehov Ruppin, Rehov Binyamin Mitudela, the Kidron Valley, Jericho, Horvat Thala, Nazareth, Qiryat Tiv'on, and Huqoq. More often than not they are found on the shelf around the central depression. Cooking pots appear in both closed and open types. The closed type has a rounded shoulder and an everted rim with two handles on opposite sides. The open type is sharply carinated at the shoulder, with an everted rim and two handles. The ware is red, and the entire body of the vessel in ribbed; the base is round. These characteristics are typical of cooking vessels from the early Roman period and are familiar from domestic contexts.[38]

The presence of cooking pots in Jewish tomb chambers has often been passed over with little or no comment in the literature. Excavation reports, for example, frequently comment that cooking pots are among the small finds and offer careful classification of their ceramic typology and date. The process by which those pots might have come to be deposited in the tomb, however, is often not remarked upon. This omission is understandable, since the purpose of a report is first and foremost to publish the archaeological data. Many interpretive matters must be left for subsequent discussion. Yet even in the secondary literature the frequency of cooking pots in Jewish tombs from early Roman Palestine has not often received serious consideration. Amos Kloner's dissertation on the necropolis of Jerusalem during the Second Temple period is an exception.

In summarizing the ceramic vessels typically found in these tombs, Kloner rightly argues that cooking pots, along with assorted bowls and cups, are "found in most of the caves. These were definitely not used for food or meals for the mourners as these were not held in the caves. . . ."[39] Kloner goes on to suggest that the bowls, cups, and cooking pots may have been personal items of the deceased that were deposited in the tomb by grieving relatives. Weighing against this suggestion is the fact that these artifacts are not typically located in close proximity to a particular corpse or burial niche. They are not found, for example, within burial containers, as is often the case with personal effects such as inkwells, jewelry, combs, or sandals. Nor is a specific connection between these vessels and a particular deceased person visible in any other way. The pots, bowls, and cups found in Jewish tombs of this region and period are the common pottery of ordinary domestic life. They would not have been the personal property of any particular person, nor are they likely to have had distinctive sentimental significance to any specific family member. They do not appear to be personal effects.

They do, however, look a great deal like artifacts associated with a funerary practice that had deep roots among Jews in Palestine, even though it had long been forbidden by Israelite and Jewish religious authorities. Offering food to the dead is known to have been practiced in Israel during the Iron Age. Elizabeth Bloch-Smith has confirmed that in spite of public disapproval by religious authorities, it was common for ancient Israelites to bring food to their dead and to consult with them on matters of fortune-telling and divination.[40] Israelite religious authorities actively resisted this cult and tried to stamp it out, but the practice persisted at the popular level. Bloch-Smith locates the origin of official opposition among "palace and Jerusalem Temple Yahwistic cult authorities" in the eighth and seventh centuries B.C.E.[41] In the centuries that followed, this elite group's rejection of contact between the living and the dead became the foundation for the priestly construct of corpse impurity. Numbers 19:11–22, for example, declares corpses to be ritually impure and asserts that contact with the dead renders one unfit to enter the sanctuary of the temple. As developments in post-biblical Judaism made the Torah increasingly central to Jewish civilization, opinions that had begun among eighth-century palace elites came to acquire a far greater cultural weight. By the early Roman period, the public presumption of corpse impurity was strong enough that tombs and graves were typically located well outside the limits of human habitation. Tannaitic rabbis taught that during pilgrimage seasons, Jewish graves and tombs should be marked with whitewash so that travelers might not unwittingly contract corpse impurity.[42] Yet even though public religious authorities discouraged contact between the living and the dead—and even though most Jews in early Roman Palestine appear to have regarded the dead as ritually impure—like their Israelite ancestors they still continued to seek out private contact with their deceased loved ones.

It is difficult to be certain about the reasons for the presence of this private cult of the dead among Jews in early Roman Palestine, since the only evidence for it is to be found in the archaeological remains. There are no literary texts that discuss or describe the practice. Certainly many Jews in this region and period who brought food to their dead may have done so at least in part as a matter of tradition. The cult of the dead belonged to a set of behaviors that had long been customary and conventional. Participation in it may therefore have been largely unreflective, part of the "normal" course of life. Yet religious practices do not typically persist for centuries simply because they are traditional. On the contrary, "religiously motivated behavior is relatively rational behavior. . . . It follows rules of experience."[43] The Jews who left cooking pots, bowls, and cups in their family tombs must have done so, then, because in their view some form of positive outcome ensued from the practice. In the absence of literary evidence it is difficult, if not impossible, to ascertain what that positive outcome might have been. Our limited perspective, from a distance of two millennia, allows only a provisional judgment. We do know that the cult of the dead took place in private, and in a setting that was strongly informed by ties of kinship. The tombs of Jews in this region and period were relatively isolated from the course of daily life, and were used to bury members of extended kin groups together. Multiple generations were interred in the same burial cave, as for example in the "Goliath" tomb in Jericho, where ossuary inscriptions enabled excavators to reconstruct three generations of the family genealogy. When food was offered to the dead in early

Roman Palestine, then, it was offered "in the family," by one member of a kinship group to another. A living son or daughter brought a cooking pot, bowl, or cup and left it with a deceased father, mother, grandfather, or grandmother. The most basic level at which to understand the Jewish cult of the dead in early Roman Palestine, therefore, is social and psychological. The act of bringing food to the dead had its roots in relationships that had prevailed among living members of the kinship group. The cult of the dead had the effect of preserving those relationships even beyond the boundary of death. The energies that prompted Jews to leave cooking pots in their tombs arose, then, from the human experiences of relationship and loss. This psychological analysis cannot be pressed too far, however, since human responses to death vary widely, and "observers who imagine that they can see plainly into the emotions of people of different cultures are very bold indeed."[44] We can know that Jews brought food to members of their kin group with whom they had shared significant experiences in life. We can know that doing so brought them a felt sense of utility. We can know that in spite of the fact that the dead were widely believed to be ritually impure, many Jews behaved in ways that preserved a connection between themselves and the deceased members of their kin group. The exact contours of their experience, however, are unfortunately beyond the range of our vision.

The burial practices of Jews in early Roman Palestine thus constitute an array of social and cultural observances through which Jewish society fought off the threat posed by death. The social structure was established in the face of death through a sequence of rituals that began with primary burial and ended about a year later with secondary burial. Drawing upon traditions with a long history in the region, as well as more recent innovations prompted by Greek and Roman cultural influences, Jews confronted death with a coherent series of ritual acts and symbolic representations. Those acts and symbols illumine some of the important characteristics of Jewish society and culture in early Roman Palestine. The primary unit of social organization, for example, was the extended family group. As we have seen, the bodies that were placed in Jewish tombs from this region and period were linked by bonds of kinship. The ritual process of primary burial—gathering at the family home, procession to the family tomb, deposition of the body by family members—put the kinship group on social display in a visually prominent way. The ceremony of secondary burial, attended by only a few members of the immediate family, further reinforced this form of social grouping. The artifacts typically found in Jewish tombs—cooking pots, bowls, cups, lamps, *unguentaria*—are artifacts that were common in and around the living quarters of the kinship group. In this respect the tomb homologized the house. This evidence from burial practices is complemented by other information that also indicates that Jewish society in this region and period was structured by kinship. The foundational narrative for Judaism, for example, was a story about a man whose descendants were to be more numerous than the stars in the sky, and respect for the family was enshrined in the moral of Jewish civilization: "Honor your father and mother." Jews in early Roman Palestine routinely identified themselves in legal documents and inscriptions as "X, son/daughter of Y," and they typically lived in housing units organized around extended family groups.

In the social structure of early Roman Palestine, then, kinship was certainly one of the most important (if not *the* most important) of social institutions. The obligations of family relationship took precedence over most other forms of social connection. The prominence of kinship networks created a social structure that Seán Freyne has aptly described as based upon "reciprocal relationships within the family or with near neighbors."[45] The funerary remains indicate that Jewish kinship networks in this region and period were patriarchal (that is, men were in positions of authority), patrilineal (that is, inheritance passed through males), and patrilocal (that is, the bride moved to her husband's place of residence). The dominance of males in the social structure is particularly evident in the practice of secondary burial in ossuaries, where it is common to find the bones of a husband and wife gathered together in an ossuary inscribed with the husband's name, but rarely with the wife's name. Male dominance is evident as well in ossuary inscriptions that show that kinship networks were patronymic.

The funerary remains also provide evidence of an evolving change in the Jewish social structure of early Roman Palestine that has not always been clearly visible in literary or archaeological data. The rise of the ossuary, an *individual* container for secondary burial, indicates that Jewish society in and around Jerusalem during the first century C.E. was granting increased social space and prominence to the human individual. Under the influence of Hellenistic cultural values that celebrated the discrete human being, Jews in the city of Jerusalem began to preserve the identity of persons even after secondary burial. As we have seen, during the first century C.E., this development was almost entirely confined to the area close to Jerusalem. Jewish ossuaries of the early Roman period are concentrated in Jerusalem and its environs, including Jericho, but are unknown in the Galilee. This concentration indicates there were at least some differences between Jewish society in Jerusalem and in the Galilee. A substantial quantity of scholarly ink has already been spilled over the general topic of Judea and the Galilee as discussion and debate have focused with great interest and energy on potential differences (or even conflicts) between them during the first century C.E. Richard Horsley, for example, has argued for deeply rooted social and cultural divergence between the north and the south based upon historic conflicts with roots far back in the Iron Age and ancient Israel.[46] Jonathan L. Reed, by contrast, has marshaled an extensive array of archaeological data to make the case that a broad social and cultural continuity was shared by Judeans and Galileans. "When Galileans did visit Jerusalem," he writes, "they would have felt at home in these houses."[47] The concentration of ossuaries in and around Jerusalem shows that, along with the continuities that Reed has documented, there were nonetheless some differences in death ritual. Jews in Jerusalem used ossuaries for secondary burial, but Galilean Jews did not. It is certainly true that a Galilean visitor would have been at home in a Jewish house in Jerusalem. But if a Galilean Jew ever had the occasion to enter a Jewish tomb in Jerusalem, it would not have looked just like those at home. This difference in death ritual rose from a difference in social structure. Like their co-religionists in the Galilee, Jews in Jerusalem lived within a kinship-based social structure, but the social system in Jerusalem was significantly more urbanized and hellenized than in the Galilee. This relative difference in social structure produced a visible difference in burial practices. At this point we must take care neither to resurrect obsolete notions of a dichotomy between Judaism and Hellenism, nor to submit to simplistic notions about urban and rural societies. Certainly all Jews in Palestine had absorbed the imprint of Hellenism to one degree or another, and the social structure of early Roman Galilee was substantially affected by the urbanization that followed Antipas's building programs at Sepphoris and Tiberias. Relative to each other, however, the imprint of urbanization and hellenization was deeper in Jerusalem than in the Galilee, and the extent of that difference is evident in the concentration of Jewish ossuaries in and around early Roman Jerusalem.

Yet the funerary evidence confirms that all Jews in early Roman Palestine shared a common set of cultural norms. One of the strongest indicators of these shared Jewish values is the range of evidence showing that Jews across early Roman Palestine were respectful of ritual purity. Their interest in purity is reflected in the location of their tombs. With very few exceptions, Jewish tombs in early Roman Palestine were situated at a distance from the boundaries of the nearest human habitation. In virtually every case, the distance is greater than that prescribed by the Mishnah, and it is always of sufficient measure that residents in the town, village, or city would not typically have come in contact with the dead during the ordinary course of daily life. Tombs were usually placed to the north, east, and south of the community, less often to the west. The dead, in other words, were well removed from the circle of everyday social interaction. Amos Kloner has rightly pointed out that even in the city of Jerusalem, which featured several monumental tombs of considerable size and visibility, "the layout and dispersion (of the tombs) suggests an attempt to create a distance between the caves and roads, to prevent the possibility of defilement of the area and passers-by. In contrast to many other cities in the ancient world, burial stelae alongside the roads are not a phenomenon of Jerusalem."[48] In addition to the location of Jewish tombs, the artifacts typically found therein also suggest that ritual purity was a religious norm in the common Judaism of early Roman Palestine. The lamps and perfume bottles that are so frequent in these tombs might well have continued to be used in domestic contexts by members of the kinship group, but instead they were abandoned in the tombs. The most plausible explanation for this phenomenon is that the vessels were discarded because of the ritual impurity that would have contaminated them once they were brought into a tomb. Thus the men and women who disposed of their dead in the Jewish tombs of early Roman Palestine were people whose religious and social world was shaped by a general preference for ritual purity. Clearly they were not obsessed with—or compulsive about—purity, since they did not hesitate to enter tombs for primary burial and secondary burial, and they also occasionally brought food to their dead. In this region and period, corpse impurity was a conventional boundary, not an inviolable barrier.

The funerary ritual of Jews in early Roman Palestine gave symbolic prominence to two cultural life values: kinship and ritual purity. As an expression of Jewish ethnicity, burial practices in this region and period were laden with symbolic representations of family and piety. Kinship relations were celebrated in the rituals of primary burial, mourning, and secondary burial, as well as in the persistence of a private cult of the dead. Ritual purity was valorized in the location of tombs and the discarding of lamps and perfume bottles. For Jews in this region and period, the highest good in life was to be found in a set of relationships among family members and their God. They lived and died as if their ultimate responsibility was to love the Lord their God with all their heart and soul and mind and strength, and their neighbor as themselves.

NOTES TO CHAPTER 1

1. Susan Orr, "Chapel Offers Drive-Through Option," *Spartanburg Herald-Journal*, July 21, 2000, A–1.

2. Ibid.

3. An example of this error is the work of Jessica Mitford, whose two books, *The American Way of Death* (New York: Simon and Schuster, 1963) and *The American Way of Death Revisited* (New York: Knopf, 1998), make use of few theoretical perspectives other than economics.

4. The following discussion does not assume that all Jews and Christians in early Roman Palestine were buried in rock-cut caves. Of course there will have been cases in which circumstances prevented a conventional burial, and in those cases it is likely that the dead were interred in simple shaft graves. Such graves are not likely to have left any trace in the archaeological record. The norm, however, and certainly the ideal, was burial in underground chambers. In this regard it is noteworthy that most of the surviving literary depictions of burial in early Roman Palestine appear to describe burial in caves. In addition, a preliminary report on the tombs of Khirbet Cana finds that the number of *loculus* niches in the burial caves would likely have been sufficient to supply the burial needs of the

population at Khirbet Cana during the early Roman period. Cf. Peter Richardson, "Khirbet Qana's Necropolis and Ethnic Questions," in *Encountering the Other: Essays in Honor of Eric M. Meyers* (Winona Lake, Ind.: Eisenbrauns, forthcoming in 2003). An additional exception to the typical pattern of Jewish burial in early Roman Palestine is found at Qumran, where neither underground burial chambers nor secondary burial are common. Instead, the Qumran community interred its dead in individual shaft graves, as described by Roland de Vaux: "Beneath the oval heap of stones a rectangular cavity has been dug out . . . to a depth which varies between 1.20 meters and 2 meters. At the bottom of this cavity, the loculus has been dug, almost always sideways under the eastern wall of the cavity. . . . The skeleton lies stretched out on its back, the head to the south (except in one case), the hands folded on the pelvis or stretched alongside the body." Cf. R. de Vaux, *Archaeology on the Dead Sea Scrolls* (London: Oxford, 1973), 46. This distinctive form of burial has often been regarded as an expression of sectarian identity, but recent discoveries of similar cemeteries on the southern and eastern shores of the Dead Sea have introduced new variables into the analysis. The thesis of sectarian identity may have to come in for reinterpretation. Given the state of our knowledge about Qumran, it is not possible to reach definite conclusions at this time.

5. Tzaferis, "Jewish Tombs."

6. Ibid., 18.

7. For examples of similar tombs from early Roman Judea and Galilee, cf. Greenhut, "The 'Caiaphas' Tomb"; R. Hachlili, "The Goliath Family in Jericho: Funerary Inscriptions from a First Century A.D. Jewish Monumental Tomb," *Bulletin of the American Schools of Oriental Research* 235 (1979): 31–65; B. Bagatti, *From the Beginning till the XII Century* (vol. 1 of *Excavations in Nazareth*; Jerusalem: Franciscan, 1969); and Richardson, "Khirbet Qana's Necropolis."

8. A. Ben-Tor, ed., *The Archaeology of Ancient Israel* (trans. R. Greenberg; New Haven: Yale University Press, 1992). S. Campbell and A. Green, eds., *The Archaeology of Death in the Ancient Near East* (Oxford: Oxford University Press, 1994).

9. E. Oren and U. Rappaport, "The Necropolis at Maresha-Beth Govrin," *Israel Exploration Journal* 34 (1984): 149–50. Variations on the typical form of the *loculus* niche include *loculi* of double width, in which two corpses could be laid side by side; *loculi* of double height, in which one corpse could be laid on a shelf above another; and *loculi* of shorter depth, in which either the bodies of children could be laid or the bones of earlier burials could be collected.

10. Within this general pattern, considerable variety is evident, especially at Beth She'arim, where many of the *arcosolia* contain troughs hollowed out in the shelf. Each trough is large enough to hold one adult burial, with some *arcosolia* cut deeply enough into the wall of the tomb to

be able to hold not one but four troughs: three perpendicular to the wall of the tomb, with a fourth at the back parallel to the wall of the tomb. Other variations include shallow *arcosolia* with a single trough covered by a lid, and deep *arcosolia* with two troughs perpendicular to the wall of the tomb, with an access passage between them.

11. Greenhut, "The 'Caiaphas' Tomb," 68.

12. R. H. Smith, "An Early Roman Sarcophagus of Palestine and Its School," *Palestine Exploration Quarterly* 105 (1973): 71–82.

13. For nails and hinges, cf. Vasilios Tzaferis, "Rock-Cut Tombs on Mt. Scopus," *'Atiqot* 8 (1982): 49–52 (Hebrew). On the Jericho coffins, cf. Rachel Hachlili and Ann E. Killebrew, *Jericho: The Jewish Cemetery of the Second Temple Period* (Jerusalem: IAA, 1999).

14. Eric M. Meyers, James F. Strange, and Carol L. Meyers, *Excavations at Ancient Meiron, Upper Galilee, Israel, 1971–72, 1974–75, 1977* (Cambridge, Mass.: ASOR, 1981), 118–20.

15. Ehud Netzer, "Mourning Enclosure of Tomb H (Goliath Tomb)," in Rachel Hachlili and Ann E. Killebrew, *Jericho: The Jewish Cemetery of the Second Temple Period,* 45–50.

16. J. F. Strange, "Late Hellenistic and Herodian Ossuary Tombs at French Hill, Jerusalem," *Bulletin of the American Schools of Oriental Research* 219 (1979): 40.

17. For the course of the discussion, cf. E. M. Meyers, *Jewish Ossuaries: Reburial and Rebirth* (Rome: Pontifical Biblical Institute, 1971); P. Figueras, *Decorated Jewish Ossuaries* (Leiden: Brill, 1985); R. Hachlili, *Jewish Ornamented Ossuaries of the Late Second Temple Period* (Haifa: University of Haifa, 1988); Rahmani, *Catalogue of Jewish Ossuaries;* D. Teitelbaum, "The Relationship between Ossuary Burial and the Belief in Resurrection during the Late Second Temple Period Judaism," (M.A. thesis, Carleton University, 1997; Ann Arbor: UMI, 1998); and D. Kraemer, *The Meaning of Death in Rabbinic Judaism* (London: Routledge, 2000). For representative and important excavation reports, cf. inter alia, Avigad, "Depository of Inscribed Ossuaries"; Hachlili, "The Goliath Family in Jericho"; and Greenhut, "The 'Caiaphas' Tomb."

18. Meyers, *Jewish Ossuaries: Reburial and Rebirth,* esp. 92–96.

19. Rahmani, *Catalogue of Jewish Ossuaries,* 21–24.

20. E. M. Meyers, "Jesus und seine galiläische Lebenswelt," *Zeitschrift für Neves Testament* 1 (1998): 29.

21. Figueras, *Decorated Jewish Ossuaries.* Also Rahmani, *Catalogue of Jewish Ossuaries,* 28–52.

22. L. Y. Rahmani, "Chip-Carving in Palestine," *Israel Exploration Journal* 38 (1988): 59–75.

23. In Rahmani's *Catalogue of Jewish Ossuaries* 93 of 231 (40.2 percent) are in Greek.

24. Ossuaries do not appear in Galilee, for example, until the early second century C.E., as at Huqoq; cf. B. Ravani, "Rock-Cut Tombs at Hugog," *'Atiqot* 3 (1961): 128–43.

25. E. M. Meyers, "The Theological Implications of an Ancient Jewish Burial Custom," *Jewish Quarterly Review* 62 (1971): 96. Cf. also Bloch-Smith, *Judahite Burial Practices.*

26. For examples, cf. L. Y. Rahmani, "A Jewish Tomb on Shahin Hill, Jerusalem," *Israel Exploration Journal* 8 (1958): 101–5; idem, "Jason's Tomb" *Israel Exploration Journal* 17 (1967); 61–100; A. Kloner, "A Tomb of the Second Temple Period at French Hill, Jerusalem," *Israel Exploration Journal* 30 (1980): 99–108.

27. Since analysis of skeletal remains shows that many ossuaries held the remains of more than one person, we should not overstate the degree to which ossuary burial preserved individual identity. The famous "Caiaphas" ossuary, for example, held the partial remains of six individuals; cf. J. Zias, "Human Skeletal Remains from the 'Caiaphas' Tomb," *'Atiqot* 21 (1992): 78. Rabbinic discussions considered the possibility that more than one individual's bones might be collected in the same ossuary: intermingling of bones was to be avoided, said Rabbi Akiba, but Rabbi Judah is reported to have allowed persons who could share a bed in life to share an ossuary in death; cf. *Sem.* 12:6, 12:9. Skeletal remains show that these instructions were not always followed. Thus the Jewish ossuary was not always associated with strictly individual secondary burial. Yet it certainly preserved individual identity to a greater degree than previous forms of secondary burial had done.

28. For representatives of this view, cf. inter alia, S. Lieberman, "Some Aspects of After-Life in Early Rabbinic Literature," in *Harry Austryn Wolfson Jubilee Volume* (Jerusalem: AAJR, 1965), 495–532; Rahmani, *Catalogue of Jewish Ossuaries,* 53–55; P. Figueras, "Jewish Ossuaries and Secondary Burial," *Immanuel* 19 (1984): 42–57; Hachlili, *Jewish Ornamented Ossuaries.* Meyers was a lone dissenter: "It is an oversimplification to suggest that the custom of Jewish ossuaries reflects only the Pharisaic community of Jerusalem, which adhered to a rather literal conception of resurrection" (*Jewish Ossuaries: Reburial and Rebirth,* 85).

29. Hertz, *Death and the Right Hand.* Cf. also Metcalf and Huntington, *Celebrations of Death.*

30. Morris, *Death-Ritual,* 1.

31. S. Fine, "A Note on Ossuary Burial and the Resurrection of the Dead in First-Century Jerusalem," *Journal of Jewish Studies* 51 (2000): 76.

32. Ibid., 75.

33. Ibid., 74.

34. E. M. Meyers, "The Challenge of Hellenism for Early Judaism and Christianity," *Biblical Archaeologist* 55 (1992): 84–92.

35. B. R. McCane, "Sarcophagus," in *The Oxford Encyclopedia of Archaeology in the Near East* (ed. E. M. Meyers; New York: Oxford University Press, 1997), 4.481–82. D. Ilan, "Tombs," in *The Oxford Encyclopedia of Archaeology in the Near East* (ed. E. M. Meyers; New York: Oxford University Press, 1997), 5.218–21.

36. S. J. D. Cohen, *From the Maccabees to the Mishnah* (Philadelphia: Westminster, 1989), 22.

37. Bowersock, *Hellenism in Late Antiquity.*

38. These forms generally correspond to Adan-Bayewitz's Kefar Hananya Forms 3A or 3B (open) and Forms 4A or 4B or 4C or 4D (closed). Cf. David Adan-Bayewitz, *Common Pottery in Roman Galilee: A Study of Local Trade* (Ramat Gan, Israel: Bar-Ilan University Press, 1993), chapter 5.

39. A. Kloner, "The Necropolis of Jerusalem in the Second Temple Period" (Ph.D. diss., Hebrew University, 1980), xiv (Hebrew).

40. Bloch-Smith, *Judahite Burial Practices.*

41. Ibid., 132.

42. For example, *m. B. Bat.* 2:9; *m. Sheq.* 1:1; *m. Ma'as. S.* 5:1; *m. Mo'ed Qat.* 1:2.

43. M. Weber, *The Sociology of Religion* (Boston: Beacon, 1993), 1.

44. Metcalf and Huntington, *Celebrations of Death,* 43.

45. S. Freyne, *Galilee, Jesus, and the Gospels: Literary Approaches and Historical Investigations* (Philadelphia: Fortress, 1988), 154.

46. R. Horsley, "Social Conflict in the Synoptic Sayings Source Q," in *Conflict and Invention: Literary, Rhetorical, and Social Studies on the Sayings Gospel Q* (ed. J. Kloppenborg; Valley Forge, Penn.: Trinity Press International, 1995), 37–52; and idem, *Archaeology, History, and Society in Galilee.*

47. Reed, *Archaeology and the Galilean Jesus,* 58.

48. Kloner, "The Necropolis of Jerusalem," xvii.

Q and Death in
Early Roman Galilee

For some time now New Testament scholars have been captivated by the Q people—those primitive Christians who first recorded and preserved the earliest traditions of Jesus' sayings. Over the past decade a steady stream of papers, articles, and books has appeared, all seeking to recover information about these people, including not only their geographical location, but also their social setting, economic conditions, religious orientations, and political inclinations.[1] The opinions of an earlier generation of scholarship, which regarded the Q people as primarily Jewish and eschatological, have been challenged by newer portraits emphasizing diversity in the Jesus traditions and differences between groups in primitive Christianity.[2] In addition to their historical and theological implications, these new developments also pose important methodological questions for NT studies. For the effort to look behind and through the text of Q has been pursued through a variety of sophisticated methods, including redaction criticism, social mapping, micro-textual approaches, and socio-rhetorical analyses. It is surprising that in spite of such innovative techniques, almost no consideration at all has been given to the ritual practices of the Q groups. This gap in the state of our knowledge is highly unfortunate, since information about ritual practice in the Q groups would be sure to shed significant light on their social and cultural setting. Ritual is, after all, intimately related to social structure.[3] Rites of passage, in particular, are closely woven into the social fabric because such rites serve as ceremonial patterns for managing the continuing process of social change.[4] Death ritual—the ultimate rite of passage—is especially significant in this regard, for the ritual celebration of death repairs and reinforces social structures, and symbolic representations in death ritual typically express fundamental norms and values within the culture.[5] Thus if there are Q sayings that touch upon the topic of death ritual, those sayings can be expected to contain valuable information about the social and cultural setting of the Q communities. In fact there are such sayings, although their relationship to ritual practice has thus far been largely overlooked. This chapter, therefore, will explore the evidence for ritual practice in Q sayings concerning death and burial. Specific Q texts will be examined in order to identify the information they contain about the ritual process of death and burial among the Q people. On the basis of this evidence, an outline of the burial practices in the Q communities will be developed. In conjunction with other recent studies of Q, these burial practices will contribute to a composite portrait of the social and cultural setting of the Q communities.

At least five sayings in Q deal directly or indirectly with death and burial: 9:59–60 ("leave the dead to bury their own dead"); 11:44 ("you are like hidden tombs"); 11:47–48 ("you build the tombs of the prophets"); 12:4–5 ("do not fear those who can kill the body but not the soul"); and 17:37 ("wherever the corpse is, there the vultures will gather"). In each of these sayings the text of Q can be reconstructed with reasonable confidence, although not without occasional difficulties. Those textual uncertainties that persist, however, are not of a serious nature, since none affects the portion of the saying that concerns the subject of death and burial.[6] Even where doubts about the exact form of the original text linger, the saying can still be analyzed for its content with regard to the ritual practice of death. This kind of analysis is by now quite familiar to NT scholars, having been widely used for almost two decades in social-scientific interpretation of both the Gospels and the Epistles.[7] As is typical of social-science interpretation, the focus of attention will rest upon features of the text that expose particular assumptions, presumptions, and conventions inherent in the original social setting of the text. In particular—and at this point the method to be employed here may introduce a new element—the interpretive focus will be directed toward features of the text that evince particular presumptions and conventions *about the ritual process of death and burial.* I propose to look, in other words, for what the texts imply, assume, presuppose, or otherwise disclose about the ritual practice of death and burial among the Q people.

What do these sayings indicate about the ritual process by which members of the Q communities disposed of the remains of their dead? What social structures were reinforced by that ritual? What cultural norms were celebrated? And finally, in what social, cultural, and geographical setting can these rituals of death be most plausibly situated?

Q 17:37: Vultures around a Corpse

Wherever the corpse is, there the vultures will gather.[8]

This saying, a version of an ancient secular proverb, appears in Matthew and Luke within the context of discourses on apocalyptic eschatology.[9] In both gospels the saying concludes a description of events immediately preceding the End, asserting that just as circling vultures betray the presence of a corpse in the open, so the imminence of the End will be obvious to those who know how to read the signs of the times. Its setting in Q is likewise eschatological, amid the apocalyptic sayings of 17:23–24, 26–30, and 34–35. Q, however, does not use this saying to conclude the discourse on eschatology. The proverb itself, in fact, includes no specific apocalyptic or eschatological content, but refers only to a phenomenon that was (and still is) common in the world of nature.[10] Similar expressions appear in Jewish and pagan sources, including Job 39:30 and Suetonius *Aug.* 13.1–2.

In ancient literary sources the common proverbial image of a corpse and vultures expressed a social norm that was widely valued throughout the Mediterranean world. Pagans, Jews, and Christians alike all held a strong preference in favor of the ritual disposal of human remains, and virtually everyone in antiquity appears to have responded to the notion of an unburied corpse with feelings of unease and revulsion. Such feelings certainly had deep roots in both Greek and Jewish culture. The plot of Sophocles' *Antigone*, for example, turns upon the heroine's determination to bury her slain brother, and Antigone speaks for classical Greek attitudes when she laments that Polynices' body

is to be left unwept, unburied, a lovely treasure
for birds that scan the field and feast to their hearts' content
(Sophocles, *Ant.* 35–36).

Of particular interest is the fact that Antigone fears the anger of the gods if the remains of the dead are not given proper treatment. In the Greek tradition, burial of the dead could be treated as one of humankind's obligations to the gods. Later, under the Roman Empire, the bodies of some criminals were intentionally left unburied in order to reinforce the punishment of their crimes (Tacitus, *Ant.* 6.29).[11] Judaism, too, carried a long-standing preference for ritual disposal of human remains. The Torah advocated prompt burial of the dead (Deut 21:22–23), and the book of Tobit told the story of a hero who risked life and limb to bury corpses before sunset on the day of their deaths (Tob 1:16, 2:4). According to Josephus the Jews of first-century Jerusalem were "so careful about funeral rites that even malefactors who have been sentenced to crucifixion were taken down and buried before sunset" (*Jewish War* 4.317). Long after the time of primitive Christianity and Q, talmudic rabbis were still discussing when, how, and by whom a corpse found in the open should be interred. Throughout their conversations, one consistent presumption is unmistakably clear: every human corpse should be buried (*Sem.* 4:16–19).

The proverbial image of vultures around a corpse thus gave voice to a widespread ancient norm by which untended human remains were regarded as disturbing and offensive. The proverb would have evoked in its hearers a general disquiet, mildly repulsing them with its intimation of a corpse being pecked at by birds of prey. It probably also would have elicited an inchoate but instinctive inclination to want to do something to prevent a human body from suffering such a fate. In the context of a conversation about apocalyptic eschatology, it would have carried a slightly ominous overtone, hinting as it does at the potential anger of divine powers.

From a sociological perspective, the dynamic of these responses can be understood as an expression of the social repercussions of human death. Every social system has to confront the reality of death because all human beings eventually die, and the death of any one individual human being actually brings to an end more than merely the biological functioning of a particular physical body. Death also kills the social being whom the deceased had incorporated. Death does not "confine itself to ending the visible daily life of an individual"[12]—certainly it does that, but it also removes a participant from the larger social network, destroying a being onto

whom the social network had grafted various roles and responsibilities. Every human death thus has an impact on the social organism to some extent, and the effects of death always ramify outward
through the network of relationships of which the deceased was a
part. The removal of even one individual mounts an attack upon the
whole, and the more socially prominent the individual deceased, the
more serious the attack will be felt to be. Ritual disposal of the dead
addresses these social consequences of death by repairing the damage that death has inflicted upon the social structure and enabling
society to recover and survive. Failure to dispose of the dead, by
contrast, leaves death's attack unanswered and allows mortality to
have the last word. From a sociological point of view, death ritual
is a necessity because, as Robert Hertz put it, "the last word must
be with life."[13] Social energies of this sort lay behind the ancient
proverbial image of a corpse and vultures, and they provided the
motivation for a widely shared partiality toward ritual disposal of
all human remains.

The use of this secular proverb in Q 17:37 suggests that the Q
people shared this attitude toward care of the human corpse, an
attitude that was broadly conventional in antiquity. In the Q communities, as elsewhere in the ancient world, it was regarded as only
decent and proper for human remains to receive some form of ritual disposition. In the context of Q's discourse on apocalyptic
eschatology, the proverb reinforces the impression that divine
powers are displeased, and that appropriate steps should be taken
immediately. While such values unfortunately cannot assist our
efforts to identify the geographical location of Q—virtually everyone from Spain to the Arabian desert seems to have felt this way
about corpses[14]—the proverb does justify at least one observation
about the social location of the Q people. Specifically, it shows that
there was death ritual among them, and that they were members
of a community. Their use of this proverb demonstrates that they
preferred ritual disposition of human corpses, a preference that
typifies participants in a social network that has instilled in them
an awareness of the power of social roles and responsibilities. The
Q people thus apparently knew the weight and mass of communal
relationships and interconnections. Like their contemporaries across
the ancient world, they were disturbed by the thought of an
untended corpse in the open because such a corpse symbolically

represented the vulnerability of the broader social network in the face of death. This saying indicates, in other words, that the social location of the Q people is likely to be found within the orbit of normal social interaction in the ancient world. On the basis of this saying they do not appear to have been socially isolated, dislocated, or disconnected. They could speak of a corpse and vultures, and we can speak of Q communities.

Q 12:4–5: Not Fearing the Body's Death

[4]And do not be afraid of those who kill the body, but cannot kill the soul; [5]but fear . . . the one is able to destroy both the soul and the body in Gehenna.

Part of a set of instructions for primitive Christian missionaries, this saying was placed by Matthew, Luke, and Q within a series of exhortations toward faithfulness in the face of persecution. In the narrative world of this saying, itinerant missionaries could expect to encounter opposition, and some of that opposition might be severe. Thus the exhortations in this section of Q strongly encourage perseverance in the face of hostility. A frequent motif in the theme of encouragement is an appeal to divine power, as the sayings enjoin faithfulness "by adducing the power . . . of God."[15] Confessing the Son of Man may bring affliction and persecution in synagogues and courts, and Q 12:4 explicitly raises the prospect that it may even bring death, but the Q people are to be mindful of the sovereignty of God, who numbers every hair and sees every sparrow. With its recurrent evocation of divine sovereignty, in fact, this section of Q functions as a kind of theodicy, in which the problem of evil is answered by an appeal to transcendence: "Justice may not be done in this world, but it will be done in the world to come."[16] Certainly Q 12:4–5 explicitly raises a vision of the world to come. Yet this saying is unique among the exhortations to faithfulness in Q because even though it carries through the motif of the sovereignty of God it actually stands the theme of encouragement on its head. The saying does not promise that God will watch over and protect those who persevere; instead it threatens that God will watch over and punish those who do not. The prospect of death at the hands of persecutors is trumped by the vision of a still more dreadful fate at the hands of "the one who is able to destroy both the soul and the body in Gehenna." The saying thus warrants faithful courage in this world by drawing a picture of potential judgment in the next world. Q 12:4–5 is powered, in other words, by its portrait of the afterlife.

The color and content of that portrait are Jewish and Palestinian. *Gehenna*, for example, is a Palestinian Jewish term that appears in the Apocrypha, Pseudepigrapha, and New Testament, but never in the Septuagint, Philo, Josephus, or any other Greek literature.[17] Arising within early Judaism, especially in apocalyptic documents that depict the torments of future judgment, the concept of *gehenna* (Heb., *gehinnom*) had its origin in Israelite memories of ancient events in the Valley of Hinnom outside of Jerusalem. In the days of Jeremiah this valley had reportedly been the site of sacrifices—including human sacrifices—to the Canaanite god Molech (Jer 7:31; 19:4–5). "Forever tainted as a center for the worship of a false god, and possibly the sacrifice of children, *gehinnom* was associated with burning, shame, and wickedness."[18] On this basis, as Jewish apocalypticism developed during the intertestamental period, *gehenna* evolved into a place of fiery eschatological judgment where the wicked will be tormented for their sins (*Sib. Or.* 1.103, e.g.). All of the New Testament occurrences of the word are consistent with this meaning, and speculation about the precise form of judgment in *gehenna* continued throughout the rabbinic period (*m. 'Abot* 1.5; *m. Qidd.* 4.14; *b. Ber.* 28b).[19] The Jewish coloring of this portrait of the afterlife is also evident in the phrase *kai psychēn kai sōma* which implies that both body and soul will be destroyed in *gehenna*. Greek and Roman concepts of the human being tended to regard death as the separation of an incorporeal spirit from a physical body, with only the spirit entering into the underworld. Israelite conceptions of death, by contrast, emphasized the unity of body and *nephesh* even after death.[20] Q 12:5 privileges this traditionally Jewish view of the afterlife by preserving the eschatological unity of body and soul, both of which can be destroyed in *gehenna*.[21]

Beliefs about the afterlife support the ritual process of death by providing a picture of the place toward which the deceased is moving and in which he or she is about to take up residence. The ritual process of death gives symbolic representation to a mythological passage of the deceased out of the world of the living and into the world of the dead. In this way death ritual enacts "a double process of disintegration and of synthesis,"[22] removing the deceased from the society of the living (disintegration) and relocating them among the dead (synthesis). Peter Metcalf and Richard Huntington have shown that concepts of the afterlife help to shape the specific forms in which funerary ritual is acted out, so that the precise details of ritual treatment of the corpse often give symbolic representation to prevailing beliefs about the afterlife.[23] The correlation between ritual practice and the afterlife is sometimes so strong, in fact, that anthropologists are occasionally able to derive a culture's beliefs about the afterlife from an analysis of its death ritual.

In the light of these observations, Q 12:4–5 indicates that death ritual among the Q people would have given symbolic expression to the belief that evildoers face the prospect of judgment after death, and that both soul and body enter into the afterlife together. Burial practices in the Q communities would have been shaped by these ideas. On this basis we can safely rule out the possibility that the Q people practiced any death ritual that symbolically severed the eschatological connection between body and soul. In addition, Q 12:4–5 has also provided our first indication of a geographical location for the Q people: they are (not surprisingly) most likely to be found among Jews in Palestine.

Q 11:44: Unseen Tombs

> Woe to you [Pharisees], for you [are like] indistinct tombs,
> and people walking on top are unaware.

One of the more difficult texts in the reconstruction of Q, this saying is presented in very different forms and settings by Matthew and Luke. In Matt 23:1–36 Jesus pronounces a series of "woes" in a public discourse in Jerusalem during the closing days of his life, while in Luke 11:37–54 the discourse takes place at dinner in a Pharisee's home. Clearly each evangelist has fashioned a setting for this Q material. The reconstruction of Q is complicated by the fact that the two versions of the saying employ different vocabulary in order to make different assertions. Both link Pharisees with places that hold the remains of the dead, but Matt 23:27–28 compares

Pharisees with "whitewashed tombs" and condemns them for hypocrisy, while Luke 11:44 compares Pharisees with "hidden tombs" and accuses them of ritual impurity. Literary critical considerations suggest that Luke has preserved the text of Q more closely than Matthew.[24] Luke's narrative setting—dinner in the home of a Pharisee—is more closely linked with the preceding sayings about purifying the cup in Q 11:39b–41.[25] In addition, the Matthean form of the saying stands within a longer discourse in which Matthew is known to have worked freely with Q material. Matthew's version is thus best understood as an elaboration on the text of Q.[26]

The original saying drew an analogy from a "hidden" or "unseen" tomb, an analogy that—following the exclamation "woe!"—certainly carried a negative connotation.[27] In the social world of this saying, it is lamentable for unsuspecting people to walk over hidden tombs. More precisely, it is lamentable for anyone to be analogous to a hidden tomb. Further, the force of the analogy is apparently obvious, since Q does not offer any explanation or justification in support of it. The text presupposes that its audience will understand cultural norms that remain implicit. In the Q communities, it could be taken for granted that people would know that the act of walking over a hidden tomb would be regrettable. It could also be taken for granted that people would know why.

Beliefs about tombs and the dead address critical social problems and conflicts brought on by death. The loss of a member confronts the social system with a series of pressing issues: Who will inherit the deceased's property? What will become of his or her sexual partner? Can or should the living continue to have any contact with the deceased after death and burial? Customs that discourage contact with the dead—such as beliefs that tombs and graves are dangerous or impure—answer these questions by extinguishing the social persona of the deceased and terminating the social roles and responsibilities that he or she had previously held. Relationships end, property changes hands, and mates find new partners. Some cultures—such as those that practice ancestor worship—allow for ongoing contact between the living and the dead, so that deceased family members can and do retain significant roles in society. Other cultures, by contrast, completely dissolve the social persona of the deceased and reassign all of his or her social privileges and responsibilities. This social dissolution is often reinforced by prohibitions against further contact between the living and the dead. In such cultures notions of impurity or danger around tombs and the dead are not uncommon. Among the Olo Ngaju, a tribe in western Borneo, for example, the grave of the deceased is believed to be surrounded by an impure cloud that pollutes everything it touches: those who come in contact with it are struck by a "petrifying thunderbolt."[28] Even the property of the deceased is temporarily contaminated. Such beliefs drive the final nail into the coffin of the social persona of the deceased and permanently separate him or her from the society of the living. As Metcalf and Huntington put it: "The fear that death engenders turns upon the extinction of a social person. What appears at first sight to be a statement about the corpse is in reality an explanation that relates the dead to the living. . . . [It is a] disentanglement of the living and the deceased."[29] From this sociological perspective, beliefs about corpses and tombs are social markers that define the terms for acceptable relations between the living and the dead. They trace the outlines of a desired social order, for "pure" and "impure" are adjectives that create, build, and organize a world.[30] As such, concepts of fear and danger around the human corpse, or the grave that holds it, trace the boundary of a social order, delimit the range of a social network, and inscribe the circumference of acceptable social interaction. When contact with the dead is socially disapproved, corpses and tombs are dangerous and impure.

The analogy of a "hidden tomb" in Q 11:44 shows that the Q people belonged to a cultural tradition in which corpses and tombs were believed to be impure. The presumption of the saying is that something regrettable will happen to the person who unwittingly walks over a hidden tomb or grave. This presumption lends further support to our earlier impression that the Q communities were located among Jews in Palestine, for the Jews of early Roman Palestine stood within a long cultural tradition of corpse impurity. Both their ancestors and their descendants placed human corpses beyond the limit of a social boundary that separated the living from the dead. Corpse impurity was enshrined in the Torah at Num 19:11–22, where contact with the dead is said to cause an impurity lasting for seven days. This sacred text closes with a word of warning that proved to be highly influential over the following centuries: corpse impurity is contagious. "Whatever the unclean person touches shall be unclean, and anyone who touches it shall be unclean until evening" (Num 19:22). Corpse impurity is capable of transmitting itself indirectly, so that contaminated persons become contaminators who leave an infectious stain on everything they touch. The Mishnah displays the extent to which this belief would develop in later rabbinic circles. An entire tractate (*m. 'Ohal.*) is devoted to the question of how far corpse impurity can travel, and by what means. The rabbis concluded that it can travel almost indefinitely, especially if nothing gets in its way. Direct physical contact is not necessary: corpse impurity can radiate outward across shadows and through tiny openings. If, for example, someone walks so near a grave that his or her shadow falls upon it, corpse impurity instantly courses from the ground through the shadow and onto that person. As *m.'Ohal.* 2:4 puts it: "The stone that seals a grave and its buttressing stone convey uncleanness by contact and by overshadowing." During a funeral procession, if a pallbearer's shadow passes over the vent of an oven from a nearby house, impurity runs from the corpse through the pallbearer's shadow and into the vent, through which it could permeate the house (*m. 'Ohal.* 5:1). Of course participants in Jewish funeral processions in early Roman Palestine were not actually keeping an eye out for oven vents along their way to the place of burial; these examples were case studies by which rabbinic teachers defined the degree of contagion in corpse impurity. Corpses were said to become impure at the moment of death, and to remain so indefinitely (*m. 'Ohal.* 1:6). Even a small portion of a dead body would emit impurity (*m. 'Ohal.* 2:1). Therefore, the rabbis argued, tombs and graves should be located well outside of towns and cities, and should be marked with whitewash annually to warn Passover pilgrims against the danger of defilement (*m. B. Bat.* 2:9; *m. Sheq.* 1:1; *m. Ma'as. S.* 5:1; *m. Mo'ed Qat.* 1:2).

Archaeological evidence indicates that ordinary Jews in early Roman Palestine did not share every rabbinic conviction about corpse impurity. Cooking pots, for example, are one of the most common pottery finds in Jewish tombs of the early Roman period, and bringing food to the dead was certainly not an activity of which the rabbis would have approved. Yet there is good evidence to indicate that Jews in Palestine did regard corpses as impure and did observe a public boundary between the living and the dead.

Textual scholars have often argued, for example, that concepts of corpse impurity are evident in some New Testament passages, including Mark 5:1–20 (the Gerasene demoniac) and Luke 10:30–37 (the good Samaritan).[31] In addition, archaeology confirms that Jewish tombs and graves from this period were typically situated outside the perimeters of human habitation in villages, towns, and cities.[32] In early Roman Galilee, tombs were distributed around the perimeter of many towns and villages, and current excavations at Khirbet Cana have identified tombs around the northern, eastern, and southern perimeter of the site.[33] The location of these tombs and graves—at a distance from the boundaries of human habitation—is consistent with ritual practice in which the deceased were relocated to a position outside the limits of ordinary social interaction. We cannot assume that all Jews were strictly observant of this boundary—indeed they certainly were not—but the evidence does indicate that most Jews in early Roman Galilee did exclude the dead from the orbit of normal social relationships. Finally, it can also be argued that Q 11:44 coheres with the typical architecture of early Jewish tombs and graves in Palestine. The typical tomb is an undecorated rock-cut cave entered through a small, stone-covered entrance. Graves, when they were used, were simple shafts long and wide enough to contain one body, and most were unmarked. A passerby might easily walk over such a tomb or grave without being aware of doing so.

Q 11:44 thus plays upon the typical architecture of Jewish tombs and graves, along with conventional Jewish notions of corpse impurity, in order to make an accusation based on an analogy from a hidden tomb. By evoking the specter of an unseen tomb, of which a passerby would be unaware, the saying depicts the opponents of the Q people as hidden sources of impurity who are capable of secretly defiling their unsuspecting victims. Corpse impurity radiates constantly outward from them, attaching itself to everyone they encounter, and their unfortunate victims never see it coming. Although the text of Q is uncertain, this saying may have been directed against Pharisees, a possibility that would give the saying a particularly ironic twist, since Pharisees were known for their characteristic interest in ritual purity. Q 11:44 thus offers a comic and burlesque image, depicting Pharisees as secret reservoirs of impurity who pass a clandestine infection onto everyone with whom they come in contact.[34]

Q 11:44 may ridicule Pharisees, but it certainly does not enlist its audience in a movement away from the common observance of boundaries related to corpse impurity. On the contrary, the force of the saying is based upon a presumption that such customs have ongoing validity. No doubt most Jews were not as conscientious as Pharisees or later rabbis about corpse impurity, but most do appear to have understood and generally accepted the idea that the dead were to be placed on the far side of a social boundary that marked them off from the living. On this point the Q people have no argument either with Pharisees or with other Jews. When we describe the conflict between the Q people and Pharisees, then, we must include the fact that a base of social and cultural continuity lay beneath their fighting words. In the Q communities, the dead were impure, and the Q people were as observant as most Jews with respect to corpse impurity.

Q 9:59–60: Let the Dead Bury Their Own Dead

> [59]But another said to him: Master, permit me first to go and bury my father. [60]But he said to him: Follow me, and leave the dead to bury their own dead.

Unlike most of the material in the sayings source, Q 9:59-60 supplies its own narrative context, briefly describing an encounter between Jesus and a would-be disciple. The presentation of the encounter is remarkably concise—"a model of brevity and lack of portraiture"[35]—yet this very short story is enough to supply a specific context for the saying. We should be grateful for that context, since the command "leave the dead to bury their own dead" would be virtually incomprehensible if it were not preceded by the would-be disciple's request. The setting in Q, amid a series of "call stories," reinforces the impression that this saying has to do with the imperative to follow Jesus. Recent analyses have concentrated upon this fact, emphasizing the implications of the saying for family relationships. The would-be disciple is told to follow Jesus rather than bury his father, thereby encouraging followers of Jesus to disregard even the most intimate family ties.[36] On this basis Q 9:59–60 has rightly been called "one of the most obviously anti-family sayings in Q."[37]

Discussion of this text has not, however, explored the specific death rituals that are implied or presupposed by the narrative

context. Interpreters have tended to assume that the saying presupposes the ritual of primary burial, that is, the initial interment
of the body at the time of death. This assumption, however, is
incorrect. Certainly the text presupposes that a son has a role to
play in the burial of his father; indeed, the force of the saying
derives largely from its rather brusque dismissal of that role. In
addition, the text also presumes that the fulfillment of this role will
require a certain amount of time: "permit me *first (protōn)* to go and
bury my father," says the would-be disciple, after which he presumably will return and follow Jesus. Finally, Q 9:59–60 also evidently assumes that a son whose father has not yet been buried
might find himself engaged in a conversation with someone outside the family on the topic of discipleship. These observations
make it highly unlikely that Q 9:59–60 presumes a social context
of primary burial. Among Jews in early Roman Palestine, primary
burial took place very promptly, as soon as possible after death and
almost always on the same day. Further, the first few days after the
burial were customarily given over to a period of mourning, during which the nearest relatives of the deceased typically remained
at home, receiving the condolences of extended family and friends.
Customs of this sort are evident not only in rabbinic sources (cf.
especially the tractate *Semahot*), but also in New Testament texts
such as Mark 5 and John 11. Under such circumstances a son
preparing for the primary burial of his father would not be likely
to find himself in a conversation with an itinerant teacher.

Elsewhere I have argued that the ritual of secondary burial
offers a much more plausible social context for this saying.[38] If the
social setting is secondary burial, then the would-be disciple is ask-
ing for the time he will need in order to see to the gathering of his
father's bones, an interval of time that might have been as little as
a few days or as much as several months. The response of Jesus is
short, sharp, and anti-family: "Let the other dead in the family
tomb gather your father's bones." The force of the saying is also
heavily ironic, since the dead would obviously never be able to
carry out such a task. Against this proposal it has been objected,
however, that the vocabulary of Q 9:59–60 does not refer to secondary burial, since in Jewish texts the Greek verb *thaptō* only
"refers to the initial burial, not to the reburial; 'gather' is used for
reburial."[39] There are several Jewish texts, however, in which *thaptō*

does unmistakably refer to secondary burial. These texts include the *Testaments of the Twelve Patriarchs*, where four of the testaments conclude with accounts of bone-gathering using the verb *thaptō*. (*Test. Naph.I* 9:1; *Test. Gad* 8:4; *Test. Jos.* 20:5–6; *Test. Benj.* 12:1,3). In addition, the objection mistakenly assumes that Jews in early Roman Palestine would have always used a different word for the ceremony of bone-gathering. Such an assumption would misunderstand the social process of death ritual in general, and secondary burial in particular. Death ritual symbolically enacts the removal of the deceased from the social order of the living, transferring him or her to a new social location among the dead. This process does not end until the deceased has taken up residence in the world of the dead. In some cultures, this ritual process is completed in a relatively short period of time, perhaps as little as a three or four days. In many cultures, however, death ritual unfolds over a much longer time, sometimes as long as a full year. The practice of bone-gathering, in fact, is naturally associated with burial customs of longer duration. For people who practice such customs, the ritual of secondary burial is not regarded as a ceremony separate from the ritual process of "burial." On the contrary, it is viewed as the completion of that process. Secondary burial is the closing act in one lengthy ritual process of death.

Arnold van Gennep, Robert Hertz, Peter Metcalf, and Richard Huntington have all found that the length of time necessary for the practice of secondary burial typically includes an intermediate period of mourning for the bereaved.[40] During the period between primary and secondary burial, in other words, the nearest relatives of the deceased are in mourning and are treated as socially liminal. They are prohibited from participating in the full range of ordinary social activities. Among the Berawan of Borneo, for example, a widow is immediately confined for ten days in a small cubicle, from which she may not emerge even to attend to routine bodily necessities. On each of the next twelve full moons she must go out into the night and recite a prayer for her dead husband. Only after a year has passed—when the flesh of the corpse has decayed and the bones have been gathered—does she return to full participation in the normal run of social interaction. During this period of mourning, it is believed that the deceased husband is making his way through a journey from the world of the living into the land of the dead, and it is thought to be unsafe for the widow to rejoin society until her late husband has safely arrived at his destination. Among the Berawan, this long process of primary burial, mourning, and secondary burial is not regarded as a series of two or three rituals, but as *one continuous process* by which the deceased husband is helped along on his journey into the land of the dead. In the light of these observations, then, it is not at all surprising that Jewish writers sometimes used the verb *thaptō* with reference to primary burial and sometimes with reference to secondary burial. Among the Jews of early Roman Palestine, secondary burial was part of the unified ritual process of burial. It may have been secondary, but it was still burial, the culmination of a sustained and coherent ritual process.[41]

Like Q 11:44 then, Q 9:59–60 assumes familiarity with burial customs that remain almost entirely implicit. The saying presupposes a knowledge of the practice of secondary burial. Among the Q people, it could be taken for granted that hearers and readers would understand this ritual practice. We can be confident, therefore, that secondary burial was a common custom in the Q communities. In addition, since the would-be disciple is presumed to be bound by his obligation to gather the bones of his father, it is likely that among the Q people the interval of time between primary and secondary burial was devoted to a period of mourning. In keeping with the social processes that most often typify lengthy death ritual, near relatives of the deceased were in mourning—a socially liminal condition—until the ritual of bone-gathering was complete. However, the particular form of secondary burial that the Q people may have practiced is not made explicitly clear by Q 9:59–60. Did, for example, the Q people gather bones in ossuaries? The extremely terse description in 9:59–60 does not indicate whether the son will rebury his father's bones in an ossuary, or in a niche, or in some other location within the family tomb. This uncertainty could be important to the geographical location of the Q communities, since the distribution of ossuaries during the early Roman period was largely limited to Jerusalem and it surroundings. If the Q people were practicing secondary burial in ossuaries, then a geographical location in Jerusalem would be probable; if, by contrast, they were practicing secondary burial without ossuaries, a location in the Galilee would be more likely. It is tempting to suggest that because ossuaries are not mentioned in Q 9:59–60, the

Q people must not have made use of them. Perhaps the burden of proof should lie upon those who would argue that the Q people did use ossuaries for secondary burial. Two factors, however, stand in the way of drawing this conclusion too strongly. First, the account Q 9:59–60 is remarkably sparing in details—nothing beyond the barest and most essential facts of the situation is described. Since so many details are omitted, the absence of any one detail cannot be pressed. Second, and more importantly, as a matter of methodological principle we can never assume that an absence from the text of Q necessarily corresponds to an absence from the Q communities. The Q document certainly did not preserve everything about the Q people; no document ever could, especially not one that was a loose collection of instructional sayings. The absence of evidence in Q, in other words, can never be taken as evidence of an absence from the Q communities. The Q people may or may not have used ossuaries; there is simply not enough information upon which to base a decision. We can be sure, however, that secondary burial was their typical burial practice.

The content of Q 9:59–60 also appears to reflect a rather intense form of eschatological expectation. In the social context of the ritual of secondary burial, the would-be disciple's request amounts to a request for *time*: "*first* let me go and [re]bury my father." The saying sharply rejects this request for time: "Let the other dead in the family tomb rebury your father's bones." The most likely explanation for this rejection is that it is motivated by eschatological expectation—the End is so near that there is no time for secondary burial. On the basis of the funerary practices implied by Q 9:59–60, then, the Q people were most likely located among eschatologically minded Jews in early Roman Galilee.

Q 11:47-48: The Tombs of the Prophets

> [47]Woe to you, for you build the tombs of the prophets, but your <fore>fathers killed them. [48]<Thus> [you] witness [against yourselves that] you are [the sons] of your <fore>fathers. . . .

Like 11:44, Q 11:47–48 is one of the more problematic texts in the reconstruction of Q, and for essentially the same reasons. The Lukan and Matthean forms of the saying are markedly different, and the contexts in which they appear have little in common. These textual problems are not prohibitive, however, because it is clear that the saying—whatever its precise wording might have been—expresses a deuteronomistic theological outlook.[42] The saying links opponents of the Q people with the disobedience of ancient Israel as described in the Deuteronomistic History of Hebrew scripture.[43] The repetitive cycle of sin, punishment, and repentance—the characteristic literary pattern in the DH—is not only evoked but amplified, as it is alleged that some prophets had become victims of murder. The Hebrew Bible, of course, does not actually record the killing of a named prophet.[44] Q 11:47–48, however, presumes that such murders did take place. Indeed, the saying not only presumes that some prophets were murdered, but it also goes so far as to suggest that contemporaries of the Q people were constructing funerary monuments in their memory. As a result, there are a number of uncertainties associated with this saying: What was the exact wording of the text, and what were the fates of Israel's prophets? At this point such questions appear to be—unfortunately—unanswerable. In spite of these textual and historical difficulties, there is at least one affirmation about the saying of which we can be confident: the saying presupposes the existence of monumental tombs in the social world of the Q communities. In order to understand this saying, the Q people would have had to be familiar with monumental tombs.

The creation of a funerary monument is an assertion of social status. By virtue of their size, location, and prominence, funerary markers and ornamentations denote the social significance of a particular burial place. The scale of this denotation is often proportional to the prominence of the deceased in the social system. Those who were most eminent among the living tend to occupy the most impressive resting places among the dead. In this way a funerary monument completes the ritual process of death by providing the deceased with a grave commensurate with his or her social status. The social organism, grievously wounded by the loss of one of its most important members, recovers its equilibrium through a ritual process that unfolds on an appropriately grand scale, right through to the end. Yet there is more to the assertion of status in the construction of a monumental tomb than merely the prestige of the deceased. For although elaborate burial places are often granted to socially prominent individuals, the prestigious dead are not the ones who reap the social reward conferred by such tombs. This social benefit is usually enjoyed by those who *provide* the tomb. The builders of a monumental burial place, who are living participants in the social system, bask in the reflected glory of the honored dead and thereby accrue to themselves some of the prestige that had belonged to the deceased. The construction of a monumental tomb thus does not merely supply a fitting denouement to the funeral ceremony of a high-status individual; it also makes a preemptive claim upon the social assets of that individual. The scarce commodity of social status, which had formerly been the property of the deceased, is partially impounded by those who construct his or her final resting place.

Q 11:47–48 represents the opponents of the Q people as claimants upon the prestige of the prophets.[45] Invoking deuteronomistic theological themes, especially the DH's view of the prophets as rejected emissaries from God, the saying pointedly rejects these opponents' attempt to confiscate the social assets of the prophets. Far from being inheritors of prophetic prestige, says Q, the opponents are actually heirs to the shame of those who killed them. Like Q 11:44, this saying inverts the status of Q's opponents: those who strive for purity are depicted there as sources of impurity; and here, those who seek to claim honor are branded with shame. It was not necessarily the case that these opponents actually built tombs for the prophets, for it is well known that this section of Q is rife with burlesque caricatures and exaggerations. Many of the images in this section of Q—blind guides, the swallowing of camels, for example—certainly cannot be taken literally. Yet each of the caricatures is based upon presumptions that prevailed in the social world of the Q people. Indeed, the power of these sayings depends upon those presumptions. In the case of Q 11:47–48, then, we can be confident that the Q people knew about monumental tombs and understood the claim to prestige that was implicit in their construction.

In the early Roman period, monumental tombs were more common in Jerusalem than in the Galilee. Illustrative examples from the Jerusalem necropolis include the tombs of Absalom and Zechariah, as well as the (so-called) "Tombs of the Kings." Located in the Kidron Valley immediately east of the Old City of Jerusalem, the tombs of Absalom and Zechariah were identified by tradition as the resting places of prominent figures from the Hebrew Bible. These tombs, however, are actually of late Hellenistic origin, ornamented—in good Hellenistic style—with prominent markers in pyramidal and tholos form.[46] Most likely they are the burial places of prominent families from the Hasmonean era. The "Tombs of the Kings" is likewise a case of mistaken identity. Located just north of the Old City on the Nablus Road and labeled by tradition as the crypt of ancient Israel's kings, this tomb is actually from the early Roman period and was the final resting place of Queen Helene of Adiabene, a proselyte to Judaism during the first century C.E. The multi-chambered cave contained a secret burial room accessible only through a hidden passage, and the tomb complex featured an entryway with a long stairway, a courtyard, facade, frieze, and columns. Other monumental Jewish tombs from late Hellenistic and early Roman Jerusalem that might also be mentioned here include Jason's Tomb, the Sanedria tombs, the (so-called) "Grapes" tomb, and the "Frieze" tomb. Each of these consisted of a courtyard, marker, facade, and/or frieze, and they demonstrate that monumental tombs were a significant presence in the funerary archaeology of early Roman Jerusalem. Such tombs were frequently associated either with great names from Israel's past, or with prominent citizens from the recent past, or, in some cases, with both.

Q 11:47–48 draws upon presumptions about monumental tombs, and funerary architecture on a grand scale was more frequent in early Roman Jerusalem than in the Galilee. These facts might seem to indicate that the Q people were located in Jerusalem, since 11:47–48 presupposes a set of social conditions that prevailed in both the social world of the Q communities and in Jerusalem. Such an inference, however, might well be mistaken. According to 11:47–48, the Q people regarded the construction of monumental tombs with evident suspicion and distrust. In their view, such activities were the work of the children of prophet-killers. A similar critique runs through the only Q saying that mentions the city of Jerusalem by name, a saying that also mentions the killing of the prophets: "[34]O Jerusalem, Jerusalem, who kills the prophets and stones those sent to her! How often I wanted to gather your children together, as a hen gathers her nestlings under her wings, but you were not willing! [35]Look, your house is forsaken! . . . I tell you,

you will not see me until [<the time> comes when] you say: Blessed is the one who comes in the name of the Lord! (Q 13:34–35)."

Q 11:47–48 and 13:34–35 echo the same theme, by which the city of Jerusalem is depicted as a place with a long heritage of disobedience and a future destiny of punishment. The content of these sayings, therefore, does not necessarily support the idea that the Q communities were located in Jerusalem. On the contrary, it indicates only that the Q people had enough experience with Jerusalem to know that monumental tombs were to be seen there, and to understand that the builders of such tombs made claims to status and prestige. But members of the Q communities responded negatively to both the tombs and to the claims to prestige. It is more likely, therefore, that Q 11:47–48 should be added to the existing evidence that suggests that Jerusalem occupied a marginal place in the social world of the Q communities. As Jonathan L. Reed has recently put it: "The Q community viewed Jerusalem as remote on its social map. There is no illusion of Jerusalem holding a central place on the social world of the framers of Q, though the claim to centrality is obviously well known. Jerusalem is now, and has been, a pretentious city . . . the Q community's social map envisions Jerusalem as forsaken and deserted."[47]

The Q people's disdain for monumental tombs suggests not that they lived in Jerusalem, but only that they must have visited the city on occasion. They were familiar with Jerusalem and some of its salient architectural characteristics, but they responded with an attitude that was generally disapproving.

Summary: Death Ritual in the Q Communities

On the basis of the five sayings in Q it is possible to sketch out a brief portrait of the burial practices that appear to have been customary among the Q people. While this description does not encompass *every* aspect of death ritual in the Q communities, the following conditions certainly prevailed: As members of a social network, the Q people disposed of their dead through a ritual process (17:37) of burial in underground tombs and graves (11:44, 47–48). These tombs and graves were not monumental in scale (11:47–48) and were not always recognizable from above (11:44). Tombs and graves were believed to be impure, and thus were probably located outside the boundaries of human habitation (11:44). The Q people practiced secondary burial, although not necessarily in ossuaries (9:59–60). The interval of time between primary and secondary burial was devoted to a period of mourning during which the social mobility of the immediate family was curtailed (9:59–60). Members of the Q communities believed that evildoers would face judgment in the afterlife (12:4–5), and that the ultimate destiny of the individual human being encompassed both the soul and the body (12:4–5).

Since death ritual is a rite of passage that is closely woven into the fabric of a society and culture, these burial practices support some inferences about the social and cultural setting of the Q people. Their burial practices indicate, for example, that the Q groups were organized around ties of kinship. The responsibility of a son to see to the gathering of his father's bones shows that family connections were prominent in the social system. Limitations on the social mobility of near kin during a period of mourning further reinforce this impression. The lineage network did not, however, extend so far as to encompass the dead, who were marked off from the ordinary course of social interaction by a boundary of impurity. The primary unit in the social system thus appears to have been the living members of an extended family group. We should expect, therefore, that housing arrangements in the Q communities were set up in units inhabited by groups of extended kin.[48]

As far as we can tell from their death ritual, the dominant influence on the culture in which the Q people lived was the common Judaism of early Roman Palestine. The custom of secondary burial, for example, had a long history in Syro-Palestine—as far back as the Chalcolithic Age—and was widely practiced by Jews in this region during the early Roman period. The presence of the social boundary of corpse impurity among the Q people further suggests a culture shaped by Jewish cultural norms, especially concerns for ritual purity, which are already well documented in early Roman Galilee. Finally, the eschatological notions evident in the death ritual of the Q communities also have roots in Judaism. Their belief in judgment after death, for example, is consistent with the most basic tenets of early Jewish apocalypticism, and their belief that the body and soul share a common eschatological destiny is consonant with early Jewish concepts of bodily resurrection. All of these cultural and religious traditions were well established among

Jews in early Roman Palestine, and they leave little room for doubt that the Q people lived in a web of significations and meanings strongly formed by the common Judaism of that place and time.

Members of the Q communities were well integrated into the social networks that surrounded them. The evidence for their rituals of death and burial offers little to suggest that they had adopted a lifestyle that was avant-garde or countercultural. It is particularly important in this regard to observe that even 9:59–60—certainly one of the most "anti-family" sayings in Q—is rooted in conventional Jewish ideas. The saying, which overturns the obligation of a son to gather the bones of his father, is driven by eschatology, a widespread Jewish expectation in first-century Palestine. This saying is "anti-family" because it is shaped by unusually intense eschatological convictions. Eschatological ideas in the Q communities are strongly formed, therefore, but these convictions have not dislodged the Q people from the social structure. They waited for the End in their own homes and in their own communities. The evidence indicates that they held views that placed them at the conservative end of mainstream Jewish opinion. We can safely describe them as conservative Jews.

These Q communities—organized around extended kin groupings, steeped in Judaism, and intense about eschatology—were most likely located in towns and villages in early Roman Galilee. It is a striking fact that not one characteristic of the burial practices evident in Q points unequivocally toward a geographical setting other than the Galilee. On the contrary, not only does every known aspect of their death ritual fit most comfortably into a Galilean context, some characteristics (for example, aversion to monumental tombs) make it unlikely they were located elsewhere. The ritual practice of death among the Q people—that is, secondary burial in non-monumental underground tombs located outside the limits of human habitation—is precisely the pattern of death ritual that was characteristic of Jews living in early Roman towns and villages in the Galilee. Many earlier studies of the Q communities have already presented a strong case for a geographical location in the Galilee. The evidence for the ritual practice of death and burial in Q only serves to increase the likelihood that this judgment is correct. With regard to matters of death and burial, the Q people have all the characteristics of typical Galilean Jews.

NOTES TO CHAPTER 2

1. For a survey of the discussion, cf. J. Kloppenborg Verbin, *Excavating Q* (Minneapolis: Fortress, 2000), 166–213. For additional bibliography, cf. J. L. Reed, *Archaeology and the Galilean Jesus*, 170n1; and E. P. Meadors, *Jesus the Messianic Herald of Salvation* (Tübingen: Mohr-Siebeck, 1995), 17–35.

2. For the view that the Q communities were Jewish and eschatological, cf. P. Hoffmann, *Studien zur Theologie der Logienquelle* (Münster: Aschendorf, 1972); and S. Schulz, *Q: die Spruchquelle der Evangelisten* (Zurich: Theologischer Verlag, 1972). For views that emphasize diversity and difference in Jesus traditions and earliest Christianity, cf. B. Mack, *The Lost Gospel: The Book of Q and Christian Origins* (San Francisco: Harper, 1993); and L. E. Vaage, *Galilean Upstarts: Jesus' First Followers According to Q* (Valley Forge, Penn.: Trinity Press International, 1994).

3. Morris, *Death-Ritual*, 1. Theoretical connections between ritual and social structure are of course based on the sociological work of Emile Durkheim, especially his idea that religion is socially constructed; E. Durkheim, *The Elementary Forms of Religious Life* (trans. K. E. Fields; New York: The Free Press, 1995).

4. Cf. Arnold van Gennep, *The Rites of Passage* (trans. M. B. Vizedom and G. L. Caffee; Chicago: University of Chicago Press, 1960); also V. Turner, *The Ritual Process* (New York: de Gruyter, 1995).

5. Cf. Metcalf and Huntington, *Celebrations of Death*.

6. In Q 11:44 there is some doubt about whether the original saying was addressed to Pharisees, and in 11:47–48 the exact text of v. 48 is unclear. Cf. J. M. Robinson, P. Hoffman, and J. S. Kloppenborg, eds., *The Critical Edition of Q* (Minneapolis: Fortress, 2000), 276, 282.

7. For a general introduction, cf. J. H. Elliott, *What Is Social-Scientific Criticism?* (Minneapolis: Fortress, 1993). For a specific example of an attempt at social-scientific studies of Q, cf. G. Theissen, *Sociology of Early Palestinian Christianity* (trans. J. Bowden; Philadelphia: Fortress, 1978).

8. The English translations of Q in this chapter are from Robinson, Hoffmann, and Kloppenborg, *The Critical Edition of Q.*

9. Among the many commentators who regard the saying as proverbial are J. C. Fenton, *The Gospel of St. Matthew* (New York: Penguin, 1963), 388; E. E. Ellis, *The Gospel of Luke* (Grand Rapids: Eerdmans, 1966), 212; W. F. Albright and C. S. Mann, *Matthew* (New York: Doubleday, 1971), 296; H. B. Green, *The Gospel According to Matthew* (New York: Oxford University Press, 1975), 200; J. A. Fitzmyer, *The Gospel According to Luke (x–xxiv)* (New York: Doubleday, 1985), 1173; and M. Sato, "Wisdom Statements in the Sphere of Prophecy," in *The Gospel Behind the Gospels: Current Studies in Q* (ed. R. A. Piper; Leiden: Brill, 1995), 146–47.

10. The etymological cognate of the noun *ptōma* is the verb *piptō*, and the noun may refer to several different "fallen" entities, including a collapsed

building, a breach in a city wall, or even fruit that has dropped from the branches of a tree (cf. LSJ, s.v.). In all the literature and documents from antiquity, however, *ptōma* never refers to any "body" other than a human corpse, and usually one that was killed by violence. This fact can help to explain Luke's alteration of Q from *ptōma* to the less visceral *sōma*.

11. Cf. also Hertz, *Death and the Right Hand*, chap. 5, "Where No One Had Yet Been Laid: The Shame of Jesus' Burial," esp. 151–54.

12. Hertz, *Death and the Right Hand*, 77. For the original French text, cf. R. Hertz, "Contribution à une étude sur la représentation collective de la mort," *Année Sociologique* 10 (1907): 48–137.

13. Hertz, *Death and the Right Hand*, 96.

14. Cf. Ucko, "Ethnography and Archaeological Interpretation," 262.

15. Kloppenborg Verbin, *Excavating Q*, 149.

16. D. C. Allison, Jr., *The Jesus Tradition in Q* (Harrisburg, Penn.: Trinity Press International, 1997), 174.

17. D. F. Watson, "Gehenna," in *The Anchor Bible Dictionary* (ed. D. N. Freedman; New York: Doubleday, 1992), II.926-28.

18. A. E. Bernstein, *The Formation of Hell: Death and Retribution in the Ancient and Christian Worlds* (Ithaca: Cornell University Press, 1993), 168.

19. For further discussion of portraits of eschatological judgment in early Judaism and Christianity, cf. M. Himmelfarb, *Tours of Hell: An Apocalyptic Form in Jewish and Christian Literature* (Philadelphia: Fortress, 1983). Tours of the underworld were also known in pagan literature; cf. Book 6 of Vergil's *Aeneid*.

20. On Greek and Roman constructs of death, cf. Garland, *The Greek Way of Death*; Kurtz and Boardman, *Greek Burial Customs*; and Toynbee, *Death and Burial*. On Israelite and Jewish constructs of death, cf. Bloch-Smith, *Judahite Burial Practices*; cf. also B. R. McCane, "Death," in *The Encyclopedia of Early Christianity* (2d ed.; ed. E. F. Ferguson; New York: Garland Publishing, Inc., 1990), 323–24.

21. These remarks should not be misinterpreted to suggest that I wish to revive the dichotomy between Judaism and Hellenism. By the early Roman period, *all* of Judaism was hellenized to some degree. Yet not all Judaism was hellenized to the *same* degree. The influence of Hellenism was greater, for example, in Asia Minor than in Palestine. Even within Palestine, however, the extent of hellenization varied from place to place, so that Caesarea Maritima and Beth She'an were different from Sepphoris, and Sepphoris was different from Capernaum. The relative strength of Israelite conceptions of the afterlife in Q 12:4–5 suggests that the saying originates in a setting where Jewish culture was not as thoroughly penetrated by hellenizing influences.

22. Hertz, *Death and the Right Hand*, 86.

23. Metcalf and Huntington, *Celebrations of Death*, 84.

24. For the priority of Luke's version, cf. Allison, *The Jesus Tradition in Q*, 16n68, and Kloppenborg, *The Formation of Q: Trajectories in Ancient*

Wisdom Collections. (Philadelphia: Fortress, 1987), 141n69. For the older argument in favor of Matthew, cf. G. Schwarz, "Unkenntliche Gräber?" *New Testament Studies* 23 (1977): 345–46; and Fitzmyer, *The Gospel According to Luke*, 949.

25. Cf. Vaage, *Galilean Upstarts*, 133–34.

26. For one of the earliest arguments for this view, cf. B. H. Streeter, *The Four Gospels* (New York: Macmillan, 1956), 254. For a recent presentation of the argument, including the proposal that Mark and Q circulated together in written form, cf. W. Schmitals, "Zur Geschichte der Spruchquelle Q und der Tradenten der Spruchüberlieferung" *New Testament Studies* 45 (1999): 472–97.

27. The adjective *adēlos*, a cognate of the verb *adēlō* ("not to know" or, passive, "to be obscure"), can mean "unseen, invisible, unknown, obscure, secret" (LSJ, s.v.). Epicurus uses it to mean "not evident to sense perception," and Philodemus (first century B.C.E.) uses it as the antonym of phaneros (*Sign.* 6). On some occasions the word also means "indistinct, unclear," (cf. BAGD, s.v.), but these occurrences are less frequent and, as far as I am aware, none refers to a physical entity. Accordingly, and especially in view of the discussion that follows, the English translation in *The Critical Edition of Q* ("indistinct") should perhaps come in for reconsideration. "Hidden" would seem to be a more appropriate English rendering.

28. Hertz, *Death and the Right Hand*, 39.

29. Metcalf and Huntington, *Celebrations of Death*, 82.

30. M. Douglas, *Purity and Danger* (London: Routledge, 1966), 2–4, 34–40, 62–72, 94, 128.

31. On Mk 5:1–20, cf. E. Schweizer, *The Good News According to Mark* (trans. D. Madvig; Atlanta: John Knox, 1970), 113; On Mk 10:29–37, cf. J. A. Fitzmyer, *The Gospel According to Luke, X–XXIV* (New York: Doubleday, 1985), 883.

32. Cf. chapter 1 of this book for location and direction of graves and tombs in relation to human habitation.

33. Richardson, "Khirbet Qana's Necropolis."

34. On the topic of burlesque, cf. Kloppenborg Verbin, *Excavating Q*, 256–57. For conflict between the Q people and the Pharisees, cf. *Excavating Q*, 204–6; also, J. S. Kloppenborg, "Literary Convention, Self-Evidence, and the Social History of the Q People," in *Early Christianity, Q, and Jesus* (eds. J. S. Kloppenborg and L. E. Vaage; *Semeia 55*; Atlanta: Scholars Press, 1992), 96–99.

35. Jack Dean Kingsbury, "On Following Jesus: The 'Eager' Scribe and the 'Reluctant' Disciple (Mt 8:18–22)," *New Testament Studies* 34 (1988): 45–59.

36. Fitzmyer calls this "the majority interpretation" (*The Gospel According to Luke*, 836), and the designation is apt, since virtually all commentators have taken this view.

37. A. D. Jacobson, "Divided Families and Christian Origins," in *The Gospel Behind the Gospels: Current Studies in Q* (ed. R. A. Piper; Leiden: E. J. Brill, 1995), 361.

38. McCane, "Let the Dead Bury Their Own Dead," 31–43.

39. Jacobson, "Divided Families and Christian Origins," 363. Cf. also M. Bockmuehl, "'Let the Dead Bury their Dead' (Mt 8:22/Lk 9:60): Jesus and the Halakhah," *Journal of Theological Studies* 49 (1998): 553–81.

40. Van Gennep, *The Rites of Passage*, 147; Hertz, *Death and the Right Hand?*, 77–82; Metcalf and Huntington, *Celebrations of Death*, 93–118.

41. In this regard it is also of interest to observe that in early twenty-first century America, the word "funeral" has a similar elasticity. A person who says "I went to a funeral" may be saying that she attended the ceremony at the church or funeral home, or the graveside committal of the body, or both.

42. Cf. A. Jacobson, "The Literary Unity of Q," *Journal of Biblical Literature* 101 (1982): 365–89.

43. On the deuteronomistic history, cf. esp. O. Steck, *Israel und das gewaltsame Geschick der Propheten* (Neukirchen-Vluyn: Neukirchener, 1967).

44. Kloppenborg Verbin, *Excavating Q*, 121.

45. Matthew's elaboration upon the saying makes this claim explicit: "And you say, 'If we had been alive in the days of the fathers, we would not have participated in the blood of the prophets'" (Matt 23:30).

46. D. Ilan, "Tombs," in *The Oxford Encyclopedia of Archaeology in the Near East* (ed. E. M. Meyers; New York: Oxford University Press, 1997), 5.220–22.

47. Reed, *Archaeology and the Galilean Jesus*, 187.

48. For a fine study of housing and Q, drawing upon both archaeological and literary evidence, cf. Peter Richardson, "First-Century Houses and Q's Setting," in *Christology, Controversy, and Community: NT Essays in Honour of David R. Catchpole* (eds. D. G. Horrell and C. M. Tuckett; Leiden: Brill, 2000), 63–83.

"Where No One Had Yet Been Laid": The Shame of Jesus' Burial

Recent scholarship has posed provocative questions about Jesus' burial, as a steady stream of books and articles has increasingly raised the possibility that the body of Jesus might have been disposed of in shame and dishonor.[1] While some scholars still argue that Jesus was buried with dignity, it is now quite common to read assertions to the contrary. Raymond E. Brown, for example, has written that Jesus was buried in a tomb reserved for criminals, and John Dominic Crossan has concluded that no one really knows what became of the body—it may have been thrown out to be eaten by dogs.[2] The problems surrounding Jesus' burial are extremely difficult, for reasons that are all too familiar to scholars of the historical Jesus: the event took place long ago, the sources are scarce, and most of the textual evidence is heavily shaded in Christian ideologies. All the same, in my judgment it is possible to reach a very high degree of historical confidence about the burial of Jesus. He was, after all, a Palestinian Jew crucified by Romans, and quite a lot is known about Jewish and Roman practices regarding the dead. In addition, anthropologists and sociologists have thoroughly analyzed the ways in which societies and cultures treat the remains of the dead. Accordingly, this chapter will draw upon evidence from archaeology and literature, along with theory from anthropology and sociology, to argue that Jesus was buried in disgrace in a criminals' tomb. Based on what we know of Roman practice and Jewish custom, one or more members of the Sanhedrin obtained the body of Jesus from Pilate and arranged for a dishonorable interment. From an early date the Christian tradition tried to conceal this unpleasant fact, but the best evidence clearly shows that Jesus was buried in shame.

Jesus was crucified by Romans, and at the time of his death his body was in the hands of Romans, so historical investigation of his burial must begin with the Romans. What would Pilate and the soldiers guarding the cross, who were in charge of the body of Jesus, have been most likely to do with it? There is a distinct possibility that they might have done nothing at all with the body, but simply left it hanging on the cross. As Martin Hengel has observed, the Romans used crucifixion not only as a punishment but also as a deterrent, and while the punitive effect of crucifixion may have ended when the victim died, the deterrent effect did not have to.[3] The impact of crucifixion could go on for days at a time, as the body of one who had crossed the purposes of Rome was left hanging in public view, rotting in the sun, with birds pecking away at it.

Several Roman writers mention that condemned criminals were sometimes denied a decent burial, and that victims of crucifixion in particular could be left on their crosses for days at a time. Suetonius, for example, writes that when Augustus avenged the murder of Julius Caesar, he not only took the lives of Brutus and his supporters but also denied them customary rites of burial. One victim who pleaded for a decent burial was told, "The carrion-birds will soon take care of that" (Suetonius, *Aug.* 13.1–2). Later, in 31 C.E., when Tiberius moved against Sejanus and his supporters, some of them committed suicide rather than be executed "because people sentenced to death forfeited their property and were forbidden burial" (Tacitus, *Ann.* 6.29). Also from the first century is Petronius's amusing (to Romans, at least) story about a soldier who was assigned to guard some crosses "in order to prevent anyone from taking a body down for burial" (Petronius, *Satyricon* 111). The unfortunate soldier loses one of the bodies, however, when he diverts his attention from the crosses in order to pursue an amorous interlude with a widow. While he is thus distracted, parents of one of the victims take the body down and bury it. The story is full of bawdy themes but two incidental details suggest the seriousness with which Romans could take the matter of guarding crucifixion victims: the soldier guards the crosses for three nights, and he fears for his life when the theft is discovered. Finally, Horace mentions that a slave who is innocent of murder need not fear "hanging on a cross to feed crows" (Horace, *Ep.* 1.16.48).

In each of these cases the central issue is an assertion of power, and specifically *Roman* power. In typical Roman fashion, opponents and enemies were not merely subdued but utterly vanquished and even made an example of. Certainly the limp, putrefying body of a crucifixion victim would have displayed the might of Rome in viscerally graphic fashion. Something else was also at work in these practices, however, something that had to do with the Roman social order. Ordinarily, death is an event that disrupts the functioning of a social order, for the death of any particular individual tears away a member of a social network and forces the network to reconstitute itself. Death rituals are social processes that heal the wounds that death inflicts on the social group.[4] By burying the dead and mourning their absence, members of a society affirm that someone significant has been lost. When the Romans did not permit the burial of crucifixion victims, then, they were doing more than merely showing off the power of Rome: they were also declaring that the deaths of these victims were not a loss to Roman society. Far from it, the deaths of condemned criminals actually served to strengthen and preserve Rome, protecting and defending the social order of the empire.

Certainly there were times when Roman officials in Judea behaved like their counterparts in the rest of the empire. When Varus, for example, the Roman legate of Syria, moved into Judea in 4 B.C.E. to quell civil unrest after the death of Herod the Great, he reportedly crucified two thousand of those who participated in the uprising in and around Jerusalem (Josephus, *Ant.* 17.295). Later, as the First Jewish Revolt was breaking out in 66 C.E., the Roman procurator Gessius Florus is said to have ordered indiscriminate crucifixions, including among his victims even some citizens of equestrian rank (Josephus, *Jewish War* 2.306–7). And in 70 C.E. the Roman general Titus is reported to have crucified hundreds of Jewish captives around the walls of Jerusalem, in the hope "that the spectacle might perhaps induce the Jews to surrender" (*Jewish War* 5.450). Josephus does not specifically state that bodies were left hanging on crosses in these cases, but that would be entirely consistent with the general purpose of these crucifixions. It is likely, then, that on at least three occasions Roman authorities in Judea left victims of crucifixion hanging on crosses in just the way described by Petronius and Horace.

These actions, however, are certainly not typical of the way Romans usually behaved in Judea. These mass crucifixions, it turns out, all come from times of acute crisis, when Roman military officers

were being called in to stabilize situations that had gotten out of
control. Varus and Titus, for example, were putting down armed
rebellions, and even before Florus's action in 66, the legate of Syria
(Cestius Gallus at the time) had already become involved with the
escalating troubles in Judea (*Jewish War* 2.280–83). Throughout
most of the first century, by contrast, and especially at the time of
Jesus' death, Judea was not in open revolt against Rome and was
not under the control of Roman generals commanding legions of
soldiers.[5] It was instead administered by a prefect who had only a
small contingent of troops at his disposal. Certainly the prefect
could mobilize those forces to suppress potential rebellion, as
Theudas and "the Egyptian" discovered (*Jewish War* 2.258–63; *Ant.*
20.97–99, 167–72; Acts 5:36), but such events were brief, intermit-
tent, and did not involve mass crucifixions. Most of the time, in
other words, the city walls of Jerusalem were not ringed by hundreds of crosses. At the time of Jesus, in fact, the situation was
peaceful enough that events in and around Jerusalem were not
always under the direct control of the Roman prefect. Pilate did
not reside in Jerusalem, but at Caesarea Maritima in a palace built
by Herod the Great, and he came to Jerusalem only on special
occasions, such as Passover. A small Roman force was stationed in
the city in the fortress Antonia, but the routine day-to-day government of Jerusalem was largely in Jewish hands, specifically the high
priest and the council, who were accountable to Pilate for the maintenance of public order. Pilate himself was accountable to the legate
of Syria, and it was in the interest of all concerned to avoid disrup-
tion of the status quo. It would be a mistake, then, to conclude that
episodes like those involving Varus, Florus, and Titus are typical
of the situation surrounding Jesus' burial. They were military com-
manders putting their foot down—*hard*—on open rebellion
against Rome. Pilate was a bureaucrat trying to keep the wheels of
government running smoothly.

Roman prefects like Pilate, in fact, often allowed crucifixion victims to be buried. Cicero, for example, mentions a governor in
Sicily who released bodies to family members in return for a fee
(*Verr.* 2.5.45), and Philo writes that on the eve of Roman holidays
in Egypt, crucified bodies were taken down and given to their families "because it was thought well to give them burial and allow
them ordinary rites" (*Flacc.* 10.83–84). In addition, as Crossan has

pointed out, the famous case of Yehohanan, the crucified man whose skeletal remains were found in a family tomb at Giv'at ha-Mivtar, proves that a Roman governor in Jerusalem had released the body of a crucifixion victim for burial.[6] Finally, the Gospels' assertion that Pilate "used to release for them one prisoner for whom they asked" (Mark 15:6) is also relevant here, for it shows that during the first century C.E. one could plausibly tell stories of Roman judicial clemency, especially around religious holidays. Thus the fate of Jesus' body in Roman hands should not be regarded as automatic. The occasion of Jesus' death was a Jewish holiday, and Pilate was not in the process of suppressing a revolt, but rather simply trying to protect public order.

On balance, then, the Romans involved with the death of Jesus would have expected that the body would remain on the cross, unless Pilate ordered otherwise. It was something of a commonplace in the empire that victims of crucifixion would become food for carrion birds unless the clemency of a governor intervened. Certainly Rome had its reasons for leaving its victims on public display. This fact can help to explain an interesting detail in Mark's account of the burial of Jesus: Mark 15:43 says that Joseph of Arimathea "dared" (*tolmēsas*) to approach Pilate and request the body of Jesus. Why "dared"? Because such a request would indeed have been daring in light of the fact that victims often remained hanging on crosses as symbols of Roman will.[7] However, a request by a Jewish leader for the body of Jesus would not have been out of place either, since Roman prefects—including at least one that we know of in first-century Jerusalem—did allow the burial of crucifixion victims. In the case of Jesus, such an allowance was likely, since Jesus was not caught up in a mass crucifixion, and his death did not come at a time of revolt against Rome. The Jewish leaders of Jesus' day generally cooperated with Pilate in preserving public order in Jerusalem, and the occasion of Jesus' death was a Jewish religious holiday. It may have taken a little nerve, then, but someone like Joseph of Arimathea could have reasonably expected that Pilate would grant his request for the body of Jesus.

But would a member of the council have approached Pilate about the body of Jesus? Or would the Jewish leaders of first-century Jerusalem have been content to let Pilate do whatever he wanted with the body? The evidence indicates that they would *not* have

wanted the body of Jesus to be left hanging on the cross. Based on
what we know of Jewish culture, they would have preferred for
Jesus to be buried, and promptly.

The Jews of early Roman Palestine had a long tradition of
prompt burial of the dead. Most funerals took place as soon as possible after death, and almost always on the same day.[8] As soon as
death occurred, preparations began: the eyes of the deceased were
closed, the corpse was washed with perfumes and ointments, its
bodily orifices were stopped, and strips of cloth were wrapped
tightly around the body—binding the jaw closed, holding the hand
to the sides, and tying the feet together.[9] Thus prepared, the corpse
was placed on a bier or in a coffin and carried out of town in a procession to the family tomb.[10] Upon arriving at the tomb, eulogies
were spoken and the corpse was placed inside, either in a niche or
on a shelf, along with items of jewelry or other personal effects of
the deceased. Expressions of condolence continued as the procession returned to the family home, and friends and relatives dis-
persed. The funeral was thus conducted without delay, and in most
cases the body had been interred by sunset on the day of death.
Once in a while a Jewish funeral might even be a little too hasty:
the rabbis told stories of people who had been mistakenly buried
before they were actually dead.

This preference for promptness was only heightened in the case
of crucifixion victims, for the Torah specifically commanded that
those who had been "hung on a tree" should be buried at sunset.
Deuteronomy 21:22–23 reads: "If a man has committed a crime
punishable by death and he is put to death, and you hang him on a
tree, his body shall not remain all night upon the tree, but you shall
bury him the same day." Victims of execution could be left hanging
in public view, then, but only for a short period of time. In the book
of Joshua, the king of Ai is killed, hanged, and then buried at sunset (Josh 8:29), as are the five kings who oppose the Israelites (Josh
10:27). Jewish writings from first-century Palestine confirm the
ongoing vitality of this ancient cultural norm. The Temple Scroll
from Qumran, for example, quotes Deut 21:22–23, and as we have
seen in chapter 2, Josephus described the practice of the Jews in
Jerusalem of burying even the crucified before sunset (*Jewish War*
4.317). These norms continued to have currency long after the
time of Jesus: *M. Sanh.* 6:4 quotes Deut 21:22–23 verbatim and

notes that Jews did not customarily leave bodies of executed criminals hanging past sunset on the day of death. Jews in Palestine, in
other words, had long regarded prompt burial as the normal and
decent way to treat the dead. The Jewish leaders in first-century
Jerusalem would have thought of it as only natural and right to
take Jesus' body down from the cross at sunset.

They would not have thought it natural and right, however, to
bury Jesus like most other Jews. For there was also a long-standing
Jewish tradition that some bodies ought to be buried differently
from others. Some Jews were buried in shame and dishonor
because they were guilty of crimes that made them undeserving of
a decent burial. The evidence for the practice of dishonorable burial begins in the Hebrew Bible. In 1 Kgs 13:21–22, for example, a
prophet who disobeys the command of the Lord is denounced and
told, "Your body shall not go into the tomb of your fathers." Later,
in Jer 22:18–19 it is the king himself (in this case, Jehoiakim, son
of Josiah) who is so threatened: "They shall not lament for him. . . .
With the burial of an ass shall he be buried, dragged and cast forth
beyond the gates of Jerusalem." Granted, these texts evince only
the beginnings of an outline of dishonorable burial by suggesting
that there might be offenders who would not be buried in their
family tombs, and that there might be deaths for which Israel
would not mourn; but this early evidence is reinforced in later periods. Josephus, for example, records a version of the biblical story
of Achan (Josh 7) and his account ends with the statement that
Achan was "straightway put to death and at nightfall was given the
ignominious (*atimos*) burial proper to the condemned" (*Ant.* 5.44).
Josephus does not specify what "ignominious burial" was—
apparently he can safely assume that his readers will know and
understand. The Mishnah is much more specific. In *m. Sanh.* 6:6,
criminals condemned by a Jewish court are not interred "in the
burial place of their fathers," but in separate places kept by the
court specifically for that purpose. Rites of mourning were not
observed for these criminals, either. Family members were sup-
posed to keep their grieving to themselves: "The kinsmen came and
greeted the judges and the witnesses as if to say, 'We have nothing
against you in our hearts, for you have judged the judgment of
truth.' And they used to not make open lamentation, but they went
mourning, for mourning has its place in the heart" (*m. Sanh.* 6:6).

Sem. 2:6 likewise argues that mourning should not be observed for those condemned by a Jewish court. Even though these sources do not always spell out in full the exact details of dishonorable burial, certain elements do recur, and enough for us to reach at least one conclusion. From the Hebrew Bible through the rabbinic literature, dishonorable Jewish burial meant two things: burial away from the family tomb, and burial without rites of mourning.

Before proceeding any further, there is a point to be noticed here about burial practices—not just Jewish burial practices, but burial practices in general. The point is this: they usually change very slowly. For centuries on end Israelites and Jews had been burying their dead promptly, and burying their dishonored dead in shame, and these customs did not change much over time. Burial practices are in fact among the most traditional and conservative aspects of human cultures, and they are especially so in unsecularized societies. When a society is still embedded in religion—that is, when religious beliefs still serve as the foundation for social institutions and customs—burial practices function as ritual vehicles for social and cultural cohesion in the face of death. As such, they change very slowly. This fact is significant for our understanding of the burial of Jesus.[11] Traditions of prompt burial, and of dishonorable burial, would have exerted a powerful influence on the Jewish leaders of first-century Jerusalem. These customs had been handed down for generations and were invested with the aura of sacred authority. The Jewish leaders were devoutly religious. To imagine that they could have disregarded these traditions, out of indifference or inconvenience, is to misunderstand burial customs in a fundamental way. Worse yet, it is to project postmodern secularized ways of thinking back into an era where they do not belong.

The element of shame in Jewish dishonorable burial is most vividly evident in the specific differences between burial in shame and burial with honor. Honorable burial emphasized precisely what shameful burial left out: the family tomb and mourning. Burial by family groups in subterranean chambers was the consistent pattern, not just among Israelites and Jews but throughout the ancient Near East. The practice of secondary burial was especially prevalent, going back as far as the middle Bronze Age (ca. 2000–1500 B.C.E.), when circular underground chambers were used and the bones of family members were typically gathered into a pile on one side of the tomb.[12] Similar practices persisted through the late Bronze Age (ca. 1500–1200 B.C.E.).[13] Later, during Iron Age II (especially ca. 800–700 B.C.E.), benches were carved around the walls of the burial chamber.[14] Bodies were laid on these benches, and when decomposition of the flesh was complete, the bones were moved into repositories beneath the benches. Over time, these repositories came to hold the bones of family members long dead, so that the bones of the deceased rested with those of their forebears.

Secondary burial in family tombs was still being practiced at the time of Jesus. The "bench" tomb had been replaced by the *loculus* tomb and repositories had been replaced by ossuaries, but the basic ancient pattern still held: bones of family members were reburied together in underground tombs. Archaeological evidence demonstrates that secondary burial in *loculus* tombs was by far the dominant burial practice among first-century Jews in and around Jerusalem, and inscriptions show that most of these tombs were used by family groups. The famous "Caiaphas" tomb demonstrates that the family of the high priest followed these customs: in that *loculus* tomb there were sixteen ossuaries, one of which was inscribed with the name "Joseph Caiaphas."[15] Secondary burial is discussed at length in the Mishnah and Talmud, and much of the tractate *Semahot* is devoted to the topic. Here too there is a strong emphasis on ties of kinship and family: *Sem.* 12.9, for example, holds a son responsible for the reburial of his father's bones. Archaeological corroboration of the rabbinic sources is found in the second- and third-century catacombs at Beth She'arim, where secondary burial is frequent and where inscriptions show that individual burial chambers were purchased and used by family groups.[16]

The element of mourning that was included in honorable burial also emphasized ties of kinship and family, and here too the traditions reach far back into Israelite history. Jacob is said to have rent his garments and put on sackcloth after being told that Joseph has died (Gen 37:34), and Bathsheba first "made lamentation for her husband" before becoming David's wife (2 Sam 11:26–27). Sometimes a specific length of time is mentioned: the people of Israel mourned the death of Aaron for thirty days (Num 20:29), and Job sat with his comforters for seven days and seven nights (Job 2:12–13). References to the length of time spent in mourning also appear in Jewish literature from the first century, as for example

when Josephus writes that Archaelaus "kept seven days of mourning for his father" (*Jewish War* 2.1), and Mary and Martha are said
to have been mourning their brother Lazarus for four days before
Jesus arrives (John 11:17–19). The rabbinic literature supplies
details of a more highly developed ritual. Here the period of
mourning unfolds in two stages: first a seven-day period of intense
grieving (called *shiv'ah*), when family members "stay away from
work, sitting at home upon low couches, heads covered, receiving
the condolences of relatives and friends,"[17] and then a thirty-day
period of less severe mourning (called *shloshim*), during which
family members still did not leave town, cut their hair, or attend
social gatherings. The rabbinic literature strongly emphasizes family ties: the longest period of mourning—an entire year—is said to
occur when a son mourns for his parents (*Sem.* 9:15).

These customs of honorable burial expose an important feature
of the Jewish culture of Roman Palestine. When they tended to
their dead in this way, Jews were doing more than simply dispos-
ing of a body and dealing with their grief; they were also making
a symbolic statement about their most basic cultural norms and
values. Anthropologists have found that death rituals typically feature symbolic representations of the most cherished values in a
culture, because "the issue of death throws into relief the most
important cultural values by which people live their lives and evaluate their experiences."[18] As we saw in chapter 1, for Jews, one of
those values was the importance of belonging to an extended family group. To be buried away from the family tomb—by design, not
by fate—was to be cast adrift from these cultural patterns, and dislodged from a place in the family. To be unmourned by one's nearest relatives was to be effaced from the cultural landscape. It was
worse than unfortunate; it was a shame.

How does all of this affect the burial of Jesus? To begin, it is certain that the Jewish leaders did not want the body of Jesus left
hanging on the cross. Instead they wanted it to be taken down and
buried before sunset on the day of his death. They would not have
placed the body in a family tomb, nor would they have felt any obligation to mourn, but failure to bury Jesus would have been an
offense against everything decent and good. At the season of
Passover such sensibilities would only have been heightened. Thus
it is to be expected that someone from the council approached

Pilate about the body of Jesus. It is not necessary to assume that most, or even many, of the council members were involved in the events that led to Jesus' death. Nor is it necessary to suppose that any of the council members had any secret allegiance to Jesus. It is only necessary to recognize that at least a few of them were involved in the proceedings against Jesus, and that they were devout Jews. In that situation, Jewish religious and cultural norms would have prompted them to see that Jesus was buried in shame at sunset on the day of his death. And to do that, someone had to approach Pilate about the body of Jesus.

Jewish burial customs, in fact, can explain a detail in the Gospels that has puzzled some interpreters: Why does Joseph of Arimathea bury *only* the body of Jesus? Why doesn't he also bury the others crucified with Jesus?[19] Jewish traditions of dishonorable burial can make sense of this turn of events in the story because burial in shame was relevant only to those criminals who had been condemned by the action of some Jewish, or Israelite, authority. Dishonorable burial was reserved for those who had been condemned by *the people of Israel. Semahot* 2:9, in fact, specifically exempts those who die at the hands of other authorities. Mark's narrative conforms to this tradition. Since at least a few of the Jewish leaders had been involved in the condemnation of Jesus, they had an obligation to bury him in shame. But they were not necessarily responsible for Pilate's other victims.

In describing the burial of Jesus, John 19:39 says, "Nicodemus, who had at first come to Jesus by night, also came, bringing a mixture of myrrh and aloes, weighing about a hundred pounds." This brief sentence showcases the kind of problems that bedevil the Christian accounts of Jesus' burial. In a word, the Christian stories are shot through with theology. Nicodemus, for example, is not mentioned in any other Christian story about the burial, but he figures prominently in the Gospel of John, both in the burial story and in his late-night conversation with Jesus in chapter 2. His appearance in the burial narrative has been linked to a specific theological agenda in the Fourth Gospel: he represents those who believe but do not openly declare their faith in Jesus.[20] In addition, the reference to "a hundred pounds" of spices is also problematic. That much myrrh and aloes would "fill a considerable space in the tomb and smother the corpse under a mound."[21] This exorbitant

quantity of spices, however, can also be linked to a theological
interest, since ancient texts often depict extravagant preparations
for the burials of important people. In both of these cases, John has
added details that advance a theological purpose, and that in a nut-
shell is the basic historical problem with the burial narratives.
These texts stand at the intersection between the death of Jesus
and his resurrection, and as such they are thickly woven with
expressions of early Christian theology.

It is tempting to try to solve this problem in one of two ways.
First, it is possible to try to identify a pre-Gospel tradition which
underlies and precedes the written Gospels, and which can then be
used to bypass the difficulties of the written Gospel narratives.
Raymond E. Brown offers just such a reconstruction in his magis-
terial work, *The Death of the Messiah*. The results are often persua-
sive, as for example when Brown argues that the pre-Gospel
tradition probably included the designation that Jesus was buried
on "the day of preparation."[22] Yet reservations about such conclusions will always persist, since any effort to recover a pre-Gospel
tradition is inevitably beset by intractable theoretical problems.
We simply do not know enough about oral tradition in general, or
about the pre-Gospel burial tradition in particular, to speak with
confidence in this area. In the absence of any external confirmation
it is practically impossible for us to know what preceded the burial
narrative in the Gospel of Mark.

It is also tempting to go to the opposite extreme and conclude
that the Christian accounts of Jesus' burial contain no historically
useful information at all. John Dominic Crossan argued for this
view in *Who Killed Jesus?* Setting the burial texts against the background of early Jewish and Christian polemics, Crossan has
asserted that the Gospels tell us absolutely nothing reliable about
the fate of Jesus' body: "The burial stories are hope and hyperbole
expanded into apologetics and polemics."[23] Certainly there are
elements in the burial texts that express Christian hope—
Nicodemus, for one—and there are elements that obviously derive
from Christian apologetics—the guard at the tomb, for another. Be
that as it may, *Who Killed Jesus?* still reads like an exercise in
throwing the baby out with the bath water. Even if everything in
all the burial narratives has been constructed entirely from
Christian theology and apologetics, these texts could still be

instructive. It is precisely by looking closely at the ways in which Christian theology has shaped these stories—what has been changed, what has been emphasized, and (most especially) what has been presupposed and even tacitly admitted—that we can turn up a revealing clue about the historical circumstances of Jesus' burial.

I refer, of course, to the well-known fact that the Gospels embellish and glamorize the burial of Jesus. Many scholars have already commented on this tendency in the Gospels.[24] Because he held such a prominent place in the worship of early Christians, their stories naturally seek to refine, polish, and beautify the circumstances of his interment. A few bottles of ointment might suffice for washing an ordinary corpse, but for Jesus, no less than one hundred pounds will do. Examples of this sort can be repeated several times over. It is not necessary to rehearse in detail the studies that have already covered this material thoroughly and well; it will suffice merely to summarize their conclusions. Virtually all studies agree that as the tradition develops, every detail in the story is enhanced and improved upon. Mark begins the written tradition by saying that on Friday evening, Joseph of Arimathea, a respected member of the council, requested the body of Jesus from Pilate, wrapped it in linen, and sealed it in a rock-cut tomb. Never again would the story be told so simply. Joseph of Arimathea becomes a "good and righteous man" who did not consent to the action against Jesus (Luke 23:51), and then evolves into a secret disciple of Jesus (Matt 27:57; John 19:38). The "rock-cut" tomb in Mark becomes a "new" tomb (Matt 27:60), "where no one had yet been laid" (Luke 23:53). John not only combines those descriptions—the tomb is both "new" and "where no one had yet been laid" (John 19:41)—but also adds that the tomb was located in a garden. In Mark Joseph wraps the body in linen—nothing more—but subsequent Gospels describe the linen as "clean" (Matt 27:59) and claim that the body was bathed in vast quantities of perfume (John 19:39). By the time of the *Gospel of Peter* during the mid-second century C.E., Christians were going so far as to assert that Jesus had been sumptuously buried in the family tomb of one of Jerusalem's most powerful and wealthy families. The tendency of this tradition is unmistakable, and Crossan is right to describe it as "damage control."[25]

In view of this clear tendency, one characteristic of the burial narratives stands out as strikingly significant: *the canonical gospels*

depict Jesus' burial as shameful. Even though they take obvious steps
to dignify the burial of Jesus, these documents still depict a burial
that a Jew in early Roman Palestine would have recognized as dishonorable. For in every gospel up to the *Gospel of Peter,* Jesus is not
buried in a family tomb, and he is not mourned. This fact is both
surprising and revealing. It is surprising because it shows that
even with all their embellishments and improvements, there was a
limit beyond which the early stages of the tradition would not go.
Raymond E. Brown, for example, has demonstrated that the burial
described in the Gospel of Mark is a dishonorable burial at the
hands of a Torah-observant council member.[26] In keeping with
Jewish custom, Joseph of Arimathea buries the body at sunset, probably in a tomb reserved for criminals. What has been shown for
Mark holds true for the other canonical burial narratives as well.
The story is steadily improved upon, but the two defining marks of
shame continue and persist: no family tomb, and no mourning. A
detail added by Matthew, Luke, and John is particularly revealing in
this regard. The tomb of Jesus, they all say, is new, "where not one
had yet been laid" (Matt 27:60; Luke 23:3; John 19:43). Many scholars have noted that this description lends dignity to Jesus' burial
because it clearly differentiates his resting place from a criminals'
burial place like the ones mentioned in the Mishnah. But as both
David Daube and Josef Blinzler have pointed out, a new tomb
would still be a shameful place of interment.[27] In fact a new tomb,
never before used by sinner or saint, would be the only culturally
acceptable alternative to a criminals' burial place, for it would be
the only other way to preserve the boundary of shame that separated Jesus from his people. By putting him alone in a new tomb,
Matthew, Luke, and John do not deny the shame of Jesus' burial;
they merely spare him the disgrace of being placed in a criminals'
tomb. A residue of shame still clings to him as an executed convict.

Rites of mourning are absent from these narratives as well.
When Jesus dies, no one sits *shiv'ah*: a few women merely note the
location of the tomb, and later visit it after the Sabbath. They go
there, however, not to mourn, but merely to anoint the body or "to
see the tomb." The omission of mourning from the canonical
gospels is significant because in other contexts all four of these
gospels have clear depictions of the initial stages of mourning for
the dead. Resuscitation stories like the raising of Jairus's daughter

(Mark 5:21–43), for example, or the Lazarus narrative (John 11:1–44) include explicit depictions of typical Jewish rituals of mourning. Indeed, in each of these stories the portrayal of mourning actually serves to heighten the narrative impact of the miracle by establishing that the unfortunate victim is truly dead, beyond all human help. Clearly these writers knew how to depict mourning for the dead and were willing to do so when it would advance the point of their story. What a shame that they did not put any such depictions in their stories of Jesus' burial.

Contradictions against Jewish practices of dishonorable burial first appear in *Gospel of Peter*, which both places Jesus in a family tomb and depicts specific acts of mourning. According to *Gos. Pet.* 6:22, for example, Joseph of Arimathea washes the body of Jesus, wraps it linen, and places it in "his own tomb"—nothing about newness here—which was called "Joseph's Garden." Later, women come to the tomb with the stated intention of performing the customary rites of mourning for the dead (*eiōthesan poiein*; *Gos. Pet.* 12:52). True, the Jews are said to have prevented such mourning on the day of Jesus' crucifixion, but the women resolutely intend to mourn after the Sabbath (*kai nun epi tou mnēmatos autou poiēsōmen tauta*; *Gos. Pet.* 12:53). They determine not to confine their grieving to the privacy of their own hearts: they will do "what ought to be done"(*ta opheilomena*; *Gos. Pet.* 12:54). With these depictions the tradition of Jesus' burial has turned a corner, crossing the boundaries of Jewish custom and making the burial of Jesus honorable.

In the early stages of the written tradition, then, culturally appropriate efforts were made to dignify the burial of Jesus. To that end, the canonical gospels tell stories about a member of the Sanhedrin named Joseph of Arimathea, a new tomb, clean linen, and large amounts of perfume. Specific mention of either a criminals' burial place or rites of mourning is, however, discreetly avoided. Not until the *Gospel of Peter* are these stories embellished to the point that they denied what an earlier generation of Christians had tacitly admitted: Jesus had been buried in shame.

This analysis is consistent with a fact that can all too easily get lost in the confusing shuffle of the burial narratives: the people who first told this story were Jews from first-century Palestine. The earliest layers of the gospel tradition originated in first-century Palestine—certainly Matthew and possibly also Mark and

John were written there—and as such these early stories of Jesus'
burial were necessarily shaped by the burial practices of that place
and time, customs that belonged to the contemporary social system and the prevailing cultural landscape. The earliest Christians
lived and died by these customs, most of the time rather unreflec-
tively, and their narratives inevitably presupposed them. From a
distance of twenty centuries we can now imagine all kinds of reasons why their stories might have taken the shape they did. There
are, for example, possible answers in literary criticism: perhaps the
shameful burial completes the ongoing conflict between Jesus and
the Jewish leaders in Matthew, or maybe it is Mark's final statement on the cost of discipleship. In contrast, an ideological explanation will be more plausible to some: perhaps women *did* mourn
the death of Jesus, but male gospel writers, suspicious of what
might happen if women began meeting in groups, expunged them
from the written record. Frankly, all sorts of possibilities suggest
themselves, none of which played any role at all in first-century
Palestine. In that place and time, the answer was not so complicated. A story about the honorable burial of a criminal condemned
by Jewish authorities was simply not plausible. Everyone knew it
did not work that way.

Certainly the early Christians in Palestine who first told the
story of Jesus' burial knew it, for when it came to matters of death
and burial, they appear to have been ordinary and typical Jews.
Their narratives clearly display a thorough familiarity with most
of the Jewish burial practices of first-century Palestine. They knew,
for example, that bodies were customarily buried promptly on the
day of death after being washed with ointment and wrapped in
linen. They knew that the dead were customarily buried in underground tombs, and that they were mourned by their nearest relatives. And by the subtle ways in which they dignified the burial of
Jesus without crossing the boundaries of Jewish custom, the texts
show that the earliest Christians also knew that condemned criminals were not buried with their families and were not mourned. It
is reasonable to conclude, in other words, that the early Christians
in Palestine buried their dead no differently from other Jews in that
place and time.

E. P. Sanders, in attempting to reconstruct the course of events
at Jesus' trial, has pointed out that probably no single individual

was in a position to know fully the exact course of events that night.[28] The point is well taken and should serve as a reminder that a degree of uncertainty will always inhere in any effort to reconstruct what happened at the death and burial of Jesus. It was, after all, almost two thousand years ago. John Dominic Crossan, of course, has taken skepticism a good deal further and argued that *"nobody knew what had happened to Jesus' body. . . .* With regard to the body of Jesus, by Easter Sunday morning, those who cared did not know, and those who knew did not care."[29] There are reasons to agree with this sobering assessment, at least in part. Certainly few, if any, of Jesus' followers directly witnessed his death and burial, and the glamorized Christian stories of his interment cannot be trusted to describe *wie es eigentlich war* (how it actually was). Yet there are good reasons to stop short of complete skepticism about the fate of Jesus' body. Indeed, the evidence from Roman, Jewish, and Christian sources all coheres around a single conclusion: Jesus was buried in shame. Someone from the council approached Pilate about the body and put it in an underground tomb reserved for Jewish criminals.

The evidence has shown that even though Roman authorities like Pilate might sometimes have left crucifixion victims hanging, they often allowed bodies to be buried. Such allowances, in fact, were all the more likely during a religious holiday, or when the crucifixion was not part of a mass operation to suppress an open and armed revolt, or when the request for the body came from a person who was cooperative with Rome. The evidence has further shown that the Jewish leaders who participated in the proceedings against Jesus had strong religious and cultural motives for seeking to bury him in shame. Such motives came not from any secret allegiance to Jesus, but from respect for traditional law and custom. Finally, the evidence has also shown that the early followers of Jesus described his burial in terms that were dishonorable. They dignified it as much as possible but did not deny its shame.

On the basis of the evidence, then, the following scenario emerges as a likely scenario for the deposition of Jesus' body: late on the day of his death, one or more of the Jewish leaders in Jerusalem—later personified by Christian tradition as Joseph of Arimathea—requested custody of the body for purposes of dishonorable burial. These leaders, having collaborated with the

Romans in the condemnation of Jesus, had both the means and the motive to bury him in shame: means, in their access to Pilate, and motive, in Jewish law and custom. Pilate did not hesitate to grant dishonorable burial to one of their condemned criminals. Only the most rudimentary burial preparations were administered—the body was wrapped and taken directly to the tomb, without a funeral procession, eulogies, or the deposition of any personal effects. By sunset on the day of his death, the body of Jesus lay within a burial cave reserved for criminals condemned by Jewish courts. No one mourned.

The shame of Jesus' burial is not only consistent with the best evidence, but can also help to account for a historical fact that has long been puzzling to historians of early Christianity: Why did the primitive church not venerate the tomb of Jesus? Joachim Jeremias, for one, thought it inconceivable that the primitive community would have let the grave of Jesus sink into oblivion.[30] Yet the earliest hints of Christian veneration of Jesus' tomb do not surface until the early fourth century C.E.[31] It is a striking fact, and not at all unthinkable, that the tomb of Jesus was not venerated until it was no longer remembered as a place of shame.

NOTES TO CHAPTER 3

1. Josef Blinzler, "Die Grablegung Jesu in historischer Sicht," in *Resurrexit* (ed. E. Dhanis; Vatican City: Editrice Vaticana, 1974), 56–107. F. M. Braun, "La sépulture de Jesus," *Revue biblique* 45 (1936): 34–52, 184–200, 346–63. A. Buchler, "L'enterrement des criminels d'après le Talmud et le Midrasch," *Revue des études juives* 46 (1903): 74–88. H. Cousin, "Sépulture criminelle et sépulture prophétique," *Revue biblique* 81 (1974): 375–93. D. Daube, *The New Testament and Rabbinic Judaism* (London: Athlone, 1956), 310–11. E. Dhanis, "L'ensevelissement de Jésus et la visite au tombeau dans l'évangile de saint Marc (xv, 40–xvi, 8)," *Gregorianum* 39 (1958): 367–410.

2. Raymond E. Brown, "The Burial of Jesus (Mark 15:42–47)," *Catholic Biblical Quarterly* 50 (1988): 233–45. Idem, *The Death of the Messiah* (New York: Doubleday, 1994), 1201–1317. John Dominic Crossan, *The Historical Jesus* (San Francisco: Harper, 1991), 391–94. Idem, *Who Killed Jesus?* (San Francisco: Harper, 1995), 160–88.

3. Martin Hengel, *Crucifixion in the Ancient World and the Folly of the Message of the Cross* (Philadelphia: Fortress, 1977), 86–88.

4. Hertz, *Death and the Right Hand.*

5. E. P. Sanders, *The Historical Figure of Jesus* (New York: Penguin, 1993), 15–32. F. Millar, *The Roman Near East 31 B.C.–A.D. 337* (Cambridge, Mass.: Harvard University Press, 1993), 43–56.

6. Crossan, *Who Killed Jesus?*, 167–68. For the archaeology, cf. Tzaferis, "Jewish Tombs," 18–32. For two differing analyses of the skeletal remains— and two different reconstructions of the Roman method of crucifixion—cf. N. Haas, "Anthropological Observations on the Skeletal Remains from Giv'at ha-Mivtar," *Israel Exploration Journal* 20 (1970): 38–59; and J. Zias and E. Sekeles, "The Crucified Man from Giv'at ha-Mivtar: A Reappraisal," *Israel Exploration Journal* 35 (1985): 22–27. Crossan, however, misunderstands the significance of this find when he writes, "With all those thousands of people crucified around Jerusalem in the first century alone, we have so far found only a single crucified skeleton. . . . Was burial, then, the exception rather than the rule?" (*Who Killed Jesus?*, 168). The archaeological report states that it was only an accident that caused Yehohanan's remains to be preserved in such a way as to identify him as a crucifixion victim. Only the nail through his ankle provided evidence of crucifixion. And why was the nail still in Yehohanan's ankle? Because the soldiers who had crucified him could not extract it from the cross. When the nail had been driven in, it had struck a knot in the wood, bending back the point of the nail. As any carpenter (or fisherman) knows, it is almost impossible to extract a nail with a point that has been bent back like the barb of a hook. Thus if there had not been a knot strategically located in the wood of Yehohanan's cross, the soldiers would have easily pulled the nail out of the cross. It never would have been buried with Yehohanan, and we would never have known that he had been crucified. It is not surprising, in other words, that we have found the remains of only one crucifixion victim: it is surprising that we have identified even one. Crossan's inference on page 168 is misguided.

7. Brown, *The Death of the Messiah*, 1216–17.

8. *M. Sanh.* 6:5; *Sem.* 1:5. Cf. also Mark 5:38, where funerary preparations have already begun after the death of Jairus's daughter earlier that day.

9. *M. Sanh.* 6:5; *Sem.* 1:2–5, 12:10. One prominent rabbi, Rabban Gamaliel, is said to have disapproved of overly ostentatious preparations for burial, and to have ordered his body to be wrapped in flax rather than linen (*b. Ketub.* 86, *b. Mo'ed Qat.* 27b). Brown appears to misunderstand the point of this gesture when he writes that "a change in burial style is reported to have been introduced" by Gamaliel (*The Death of the Messiah*, 1243). Gamaliel did not, however, introduce any change in Jewish burial practices: his body was wrapped in cloth like any other Jewish corpse. What Gamaliel changed was the degree of ostentation by insisting on plain simple flax rather than fine linen. Such sentiments are rather common in the anthropology of death ritual. In the ancient world, Solon, Plato,

and Cicero are all said to have urged limitations on funerary display (Plut. *Sol.* 21.5; Cicero, *Leg.* 2.23.59, 2.24.60).

10. *M. B. Bat.* 2:9; cf. also Kloner, "The Necropolis of Jerusalem."

11. For the sociology and anthropology of death ritual, cf. Metcalf and Huntington, *Celebrations of Death.* Maurice Bloch and Jonathan Parry, eds., *Death and the Regeneration of Life* (New York: Cambridge University Press, 1982). R. Chapman, I. Kinnes, and K. Randsborg, eds., *The Archaeology of Death* (Cambridge: Cambridge University Press, 1981).

12. Campbell and Green, *The Archaeology of Death.*

13. Rivka Gonen, *Burial Patterns and Cultural Diversity in Late Bronze Age Canaan* (ASOR Dissertation Series 7; Winona Lake, Ind.: Eisenbrauns, 1992).

14. Bloch-Smith, *Judahite Burial Practices.*

15. Greenhut, "The Caiaphas Tomb," 63–71.

16. Moshe Schwabe and Baruch Lifshitz, *The Greek Inscriptions* (vol. 2 of *Beth She'arim*; New Brunswick, N.J.: Rutgers, 1974), 223.

17. Levi Y. Rahmani, "Ancient Jerusalem's Funerary Customs and Tombs, Part One," *Biblical Archaeologist* 44 (1981): 175.

18. Metcalf and Huntington, *Celebrations of Death,* 25.

19. Crossan, *Who Killed Jesus?,* 173.

20. R. Alan Culpepper, *Anatomy of the Fourth Gospel* (Philadelphia: Fortress, 1983), 136.

21. Brown, *The Death of the Messiah,* 1260.

22. Ibid., 1238–41.

23. Crossan, *Who Killed Jesus?,* 188.

24. Cf., inter alia, Blinzler, "Die Grablegung Jesu," 74; Brown, "The Burial of Jesus," 242–43; Crossan, *The Historical Jesus,* 393–94; Daube, *The New Testament and Rabbinic Judaism,* 311; R. Pesch, *Das Markusevangelium* (Freiburg: Herder, 1977), 2.516; Fitzmyer, *The Gospel According to Saint Luke* (Garden City: Doubleday, 1981), 21523–25; and R. Schnackenburg, *Das Johannesevangelium* (Freiburg: Herder, 1977), 2.346.

25. Crossan, *The Historical Jesus,* 394.

26. Brown, "The Burial of Jesus."

27. Blinzler, "Die Grablegung Jesu," 101–2. Daube, *The New Testament and Rabbinic Judaism,* 311.

28. E. P. Sanders, *Jesus and Judaism* (Philadelphia: Fortress, 1985), 300.

29. Crossan, *The Historical Jesus,* 394 (italics his).

30. Joachim Jeremias, *Heilegengräber in Jesu Umwelt* (Göttingen: Vandenhoeck & Ruprecht, 1958), 145.

31. Eusebius, *Vita Constantini* 3.25–32.

Is a Corpse Contagious?
Relocating the Dead in Early
Byzantine Palestine

Our understanding of the relationship between early Judaism and Christianity has been developing rapidly in recent years as ongoing research continues to uncover previously unsuspected dimensions of interest and complexity. A generation ago, studies of early Judaism and Christianity drew heavily—*too* heavily—from early Christian literature, and generally concluded that Judaism and Christianity had effectively separated from each other by the end of the first century C.E.[1] New Testament scholars in particular conventionally spoke of a "split" between Judaism and Christianity during the late first or early second century.[2] The historical weaknesses, and apologetic purposes, of these arguments are by now all too evident, and as a result they are steadily giving way to a broader outlook. Evidence from sources outside the New Testament continues to mount, and the early history of Judaism and Christianity is now coming to be seen as a story of "fraternal twins" who experienced both contacts and conflicts during their early years.[3] Daniel Boyarin caught the current state of the discussion nicely when he wrote that Judaism and Christianity "continued jostling each other in the womb well into late antiquity."[4] The old notion of an early "split" may still have its defenders, but social differentiation between Jews and Christians now appears to have been neither early nor abrupt, and may not have become pronounced in the region of Palestine until as late as the fourth century.

In the effort to understand better the early history of these "twins in the womb," death ritual is an area of research with unusual potential for illuminating the social contours of their relationship. For death ritual, as a rite of passage, is intimately related to social structure. Human death poses substantial problems for a

society and culture, and death ritual exists to address and confront
those problems. Ritual treatment of the dead rises from the social
structure, and changes in death ritual do not appear for light and
transient causes, but from significant changes in the social structure. The preceding chapters of this book have represented one of
the first attempts to bring death ritual into our picture of Jewish
and Christian relations in early Roman Palestine.[5] In keeping with
the new perspective that regards early Judaism and Christianity as
"fraternal twins," those chapters have argued that Jews and
Christians in Palestine shared a common pattern of death ritual
throughout the early Roman period. In view of this outcome, a further question naturally suggests itself at this point: If Jews and
Christians in early Roman Palestine shared common burial practices, when did Jews and Christians in Palestine begin to treat their
dead *differently*? At what point *did* death ritual emerge as a point of
disagreement (a bone of contention, as it were) between Christians
and Jews? This chapter will examine the evidence for death ritual
in Palestine after the early Roman period, with particular interest
in identifying the point at which Christians and Jews in this region
began to treat their dead differently. My contention will be that
distinctions between Jewish and Christian death ritual did not
emerge until the fourth century, when attitudes toward, and beliefs
about, dead bodies become a matter of mutual self-definition.

We begin with a conversation that, by all the best evidence, took
place in the Lower Galilee during the early first century C.E. Two
Jewish men were discussing the obligation of a son to tend to his
father's burial, an obligation that most Jews in that place and time
regarded as among the most important filial duties. That, in fact,
was exactly the point of view expressed by one of the parties to the
conversation when he suggested that a son's responsibility for his
father's burial was so important as to override any other possible
commitment. This point of view, so reasonable and sensible to
most Jews in early Roman Palestine, was met with a surprising
retort: "Let the dead bury their own dead," snapped Jesus of
Nazareth. This conversation, recorded in the Q tradition, is noteworthy not only for what it explicitly states (namely, that the historical Jesus could and did flout one of the more deeply seated
conventions of his culture), but even more because of what it so
clearly implies. It coheres in several details with the typical burial

practices of first-century Jews in the Lower Galilee. The precise matter at stake was whether the man would become more than a conversation partner with Jesus—would he become a disciple as well? Clearly he was open to the idea, but with one caveat: "First let me go and bury my father." Jesus' quick and cutting reply indicates that both he and the would-be disciple knew the particulars of the ritual process by which the bodies of Jewish dead were laid to rest. They knew, for instance, that Jewish burial was a time-consuming process: the request, "*First* let me go and bury my father," implies that after an interval of time the man would be able to join the circle of Jesus' followers. As we have seen, Jewish death ritual in early Roman Galilee did take a considerable amount of time, a full calendar year. Jesus' reply—"Let the dead bury their own dead"—plays somewhat humorously and flippantly with the Jewish practice of secondary burial.[6] Both Jesus and his conversation partner were able to take for granted the fact that the dead were customarily laid to rest by a ritual process that lasted for some time, and that entailed the reburial of human bones.

It may not be particularly surprising to find two Jewish men in first-century Galilee who were familiar with the customary Jewish death ritual of that place and time. Certainly we should only expect as much. More significant is the fact that the story of their conversation was handed down in the Q tradition without the first word of comment or explanation. Apparently none was necessary. The story could be told in a simple and straightforward fashion because readers (or, more likely, hearers) in the Q communities could be counted on to understand the issues at stake in the conversation. Other texts from the Jesus traditions show that early Christians not only knew about the process of secondary burial, they could also be counted to hear the joke in a remark about a whitewashed tomb (Matt 23:27), and to wince inwardly at the specter of an unmarked grave (Q 11:44). They believed that the fourth day after death was the point at which bodily decomposition began (John 11:39), and they understood that some bodies had to be interred in dishonor. And they knew all about the physical artifacts of Jewish death ritual: the wrappings and bindings, the perfume bottles, the coffins, the ossuaries, and the underground chambers with heavy stones over their entrances. All of these things were familiar facts of life to them. Here, then, is the point at which our study of death ritual in early Roman Palestine has arrived: the earliest Christian groups in Palestine were full participants in the common and conventional Jewish death ritual of that place and time. They buried their dead like other Jews. Whatever tensions, conflicts, battles, and schisms there may have been between Jews and Christians in early Roman Palestine, they did not extend so far or so deep as to include matters of death and burial. There may have been Jewish and Christian conflict in the synagogue, but there was none at the cemetery.

The first significant aspect of death ritual on which Jews and Christians eventually came to disagree was the social location of the human corpse. Initially, Christians and Jews in Palestine shared a common presumption about corpse impurity: they agreed that the dead were impure, and they regarded this impurity as a contamination that was to be avoided. On this basis both Christians and Jews customarily located the dead outside the margin of the social network. In the fourth century, however, the situation began to change. Explicitly denying the impurity of the human corpse, Christians began to treat dead bodies, or parts thereof, in ways that had previously been regarded as inappropriate. In particular, Christians consciously violated the social boundary of corpse impurity and brought the remains of the dead into social spaces and locations that had formerly been off-limits. Christian dead were brought into the center of public space and given a prominent role in public worship. By relocating their dead from the margin to the center, fourth-century Christians in Palestine were beginning to differentiate themselves from Jews by tracing out an alternative to the Jewish perimeter around the social order. With the rise of their public cult of martyrs, Christians welcomed the human corpse into an emerging vision of an ideal Christian society.

For at least the first two centuries C.E., however Christians in Palestine participated in this general Jewish consensus about corpse impurity. During this period "when Christians were Jews,"[7] they too regarded the human corpse as a source of contamination. Jewish and Christian tombs of this period, for example, are archaeologically indistinguishable from each other, indicating that Christians (like other Jews) interred their dead in graves and tombs located outside the limits of human habitation in cities, towns, and villages, almost certainly for reasons of impurity. In addition, as we have seen, some early Christian texts unmistakably presuppose Jewish customs regarding corpse impurity. From the Q tradition, Q 11:44 is a saying in which Pharisees are compared with "unmarked graves that people walk over without realizing it." Beliefs about corpse impurity are certainly at work in the polemic of this saying. Given the typical architecture of Jewish and Christian tombs in this region and period—undecorated rock-cut caves with small, sealed entrances, located beyond the edge of town—a traveler or passerby might easily overshadow a burial cave without being aware of it. Q 11:44 plays on conventional Jewish belief in the contagion of corpse impurity by evoking the specter of a hidden tomb, of which a passerby is unaware. In the Jewish culture of early Roman Palestine, unmarked graves would be hidden sources of contamination, and persons who unwittingly overshadowed them would be defiled without knowing it. To call one's opponents "hidden tombs" would be to depict those opponents as reservoirs of secret impurity who surreptitiously defile their unsuspecting followers.

Two other early Christian texts—one from the late first century, and the other from the late second or early third—also presuppose the Jewish construct of corpse impurity. Indeed, both of these texts presume a specific custom that is described in several passages in the Mishnah. As we saw in chapter 2, *m. Sheq.* 1:1, *m. Ma'as. S.* 5:1, and *m. Mo'ed Qat.* 1:2 all refer to a custom of marking tombs and graves with whitewash at the time of festivals, so as to warn pilgrims against the danger of defilement. While *m. Sheq.* 1:1 lists the marking of graves among several preparations that should be made annually in the weeks immediately before Passover, *m. Mo'ed Qat.* 1:2 mentions grave-marking as one of the tasks that can be undertaken during the mid-festival days. Matt 23:27–28, in which the first evangelist has significantly reworked Q 11:44, also appears to have this custom of grave-marking in view. Matthew's version equates Pharisees with "whitewashed tombs which are full of dead bones and all kinds of uncleanness." In keeping with his interest in moving readers away from allegiance to Pharisaic teachers and toward Christian interpretations of Jewish religion, Matthew has raised the level of satire in the original Q saying. In the context of the sustained anti-Pharisaic harangue in Matt 23, the Matthean version of the saying is ironic and sarcastic: Pharisees, who especially sought to avoid corpse impurity, are here portrayed

as sources of it. In spite of their quest to live in a state of worship
and purity, they are depicted as permanently unfit to appear in the
presence of God. Certainly this text can be taken as evidence of
conflict between Matthew's community and Pharisaic Judaism in
late first-century Palestine. For our purposes, however, the more
important characteristic of Matt 23:27–28 is the way in which it
presumes, and in fact builds upon, conventional Jewish constructs
of corpse impurity. The custom of marking tombs and graves with
whitewash for reasons of purity is employed as a rhetorical tech-
nique in creating a burlesque image of the Pharisees. Of course that
burlesque, like many other images in Matt 23, is garish, exagger-
ated, and polemical. But it is also predicated upon Christians'
knowledge and observance of the custom of marking graves for
purposes of purity. The sarcasm in the caricature of a "whitewashed tomb" depends upon the presumption that tombs are
unclean and so must be whitewashed.

A brief story in the Pseudo-Clementine *Recognitions*, a Christian
text from the late second or early third century, also presupposes
that its readers are familiar with the practice of grave-marking.
This document, which relates the journeys of Clement through the
land of Palestine, mentions in passing that the graves of two
Christians at Jericho were miraculously whitened every year.
Clement, in fact, escapes arrest at the hands of Saul because he has
temporarily gone out to see these extraordinary tombs. Passing
through Jericho, Saul cannot find Clement, because "at that time
we were absent, having gone out to the sepulchers of two brethren
which were whitened of themselves every year, by which miracle
the fury of many against us was restrained, because they saw that
our brethren were had in remembrance before God" (1.71). The
tombs were "whitened . . . every year" (*per annos singulos dealbaban-
tur*) indicates a custom for which the text provides no explanation
or justification. Certainly the implied reader of this text does not
need any explanation. Instead, the miraculous whitening is
adduced as evidence for God's remembrance of the Christian dead,
as if God has personally seen to it that their tombs were appropriately marked. No doubt the early Christian readers who were
entertained and edified by this and other stories in the *Recognitions*
also assumed that Clement kept a close eye on his shadow while
visiting these tombs.

For at least the first two centuries, then, Christians in Palestine concurred with their Jewish co-religionists in regarding corpse impurity as a boundary that rightly separated the dead from the social network. All alike believed that the living and the dead stood on opposite sides of a social boundary: the bones of the dead, and the tombs that held them, were impure, and this impurity could infect the living. The boundary was to be respected and unnecessary contact with the dead avoided. The public consensus on the impurity of human corpses did not stop many Jews and Christians from seeking private contact with their deceased family members. The cooking pots that are so common in Jewish tombs from the early Roman period offer silent but irrefutable testimony to the abiding appeal of the private cult of the dead.

But that was during the first two centuries. Changes in Christian attitudes toward the dead begin to surface during the third and fourth centuries, first in texts and later in the material culture. Two early church orders—the third-century *Didascalia Apostolorum* and the fourth-century *Apostolic Constitutions*—both pointedly repudiate Jewish constructs of corpse impurity and the social boundary that those constructs supported. Written in Syria, these documents "actively seek to remove Jewish practices (including corpse impurity) from the churches."[8] The *Didascalia Apostolorum*, for example, argues that Christians should not observe Jewish rituals because such customs belong to the "Second Legislation" imposed on the disobedient people of Israel after the incident with the golden calf. Christians, and Jews who have become Christians, should not observe the Passover (5.17), keep the Sabbath (5.20; 6.18–19), or perform ritual cleansings (6.20–21). In particular, they should not fear corpse impurity:

> For in the Second Legislation, if one touches a dead man or a tomb, he is baptized; but do you, according to the Gospel and according to the power of the Holy Spirit, come together even in the cemeteries, and read the holy scriptures, and without demur perform your ministry and your supplication to God? . . . For they who have believed in God, according to the Gospel, even though they should sleep, they are not dead. . . . For this cause therefore do you approach without restraint to those who are at rest, and hold them not unclean. (*Did. Apost.* 6.22)

Similar assertions appear in the *Apostolic Constitutions*, the first six books of which draw heavily from the *Didascalia Apostolorum*. Here too the argument is made that Christians should not observe Jewish rituals, especially those related to impurities caused by sexual activity and death (6.27–30):

> Neither do you seek after Jewish separations, or perpetual washings, or purifications upon the touch of a dead body. But without such observations assemble in the cemeteries, reading the holy books, and singing . . . for your brethren that are asleep in the Lord. . . . You also, oh bishops, and the rest, who without such observances touch those who are sleeping, ought not to think yourselves defiled. (*Apost. Const.* 6.30)

These statements about the human corpse are different from the Christian views that appeared in earlier texts from the first and second centuries. Here the boundary between the living and the dead is not presumed but effaced, as it is asserted that the dead are not contagiously impure. Contact with the dead does not infect or defile and it need not take place in secret. On the contrary, the corpses of the Christian dead are harmless. The reason given for this view is especially important: the Christian dead are not impure, these texts allege, because they are *not really dead* (*Did. Apost.* 6.22). They may be "asleep" or "at rest," but they are part of the Christian social network and should not be separated from it.

It would be irresponsible, of course, to assume that these early church orders reflect the actual structure of social relationships in Palestine during the third and fourth centuries C.E. There are at least two good reasons that stand in the way of such a presumption. First, both of these documents come from Syria, not Palestine, and thus they can reflect at most only indirectly upon the social situation in late Roman Palestine. The social relationships between Jews and non-Jews were significantly different in Syria, where Jews were a minority, than in Palestine, where they constituted a much larger segment of the social structure. Still more importantly, the *Didascalia Apostolorum* and the *Apostolic Constitutions* openly and aggressively advocate for change, and the energy with which they call for Christians to renounce Jewish ritual practices strongly suggests that their view was probably not the social norm. The implied reader of these documents, in fact, is a Jewish-Christian who still observes a number of customs from the "Second Legislation."[9] We cannot conclude, therefore, that Jewish and Christian social norms in Palestine were diverging, and that Jewish boundaries of corpse impurity were dissolving, simply because these documents from Syria wanted them to be.

Yet the early church orders do show that during the third and fourth centuries there were at least some Christians in the East who were beginning to advocate for differentiation from Jews in matters relating to corpse impurity. A Christian alternative to the Jewish perimeter around society was beginning to take shape, and it was beginning to appear that the Christian dead might not be impure for much longer. Certainly Jerome, writing in Bethlehem in the year 406, would be able to declare quite confidently that the bones of martyrs carried no contamination (*Vigil.* 8). *Apostolic Constitutions* 6.30 hints that other changes also lie ahead: "and in the processions of those who have fallen asleep, accompany them with singing, if they were faithful in Christ." Unlike earlier Jewish, and Christian, funeral processions, which featured lamentations and mourning, Christian corpses in the fourth and fifth centuries might soon be escorted to their burial places with music and songs.

How much things had changed by the time of Jerome, who lived in Bethlehem but not in the world of Jesus. By Jerome's day, the cultural weight of Greece and Rome had been bearing down on traditional Jewish death ritual for several centuries, and the political power of Rome had made the Christians—formerly little more than a Jewish sect—the imperially sanctioned religion. By the early fifth century the influence of those Greek and Roman *refrigeria* had worked its full effect on the social structure of Palestine. The cult of the dead had come out into the open, and Christians were leading the way. Jerome not only participated in a cult of the dead, he gave it his written approval and argued that it was a Christian duty to take part. When a former student had the temerity to question the legitimacy of this cult, Jerome let fly with his own special brand of rhetorical firepower, mocking Vigilantius for impugning the idea of contact between the living and the dead. In particular, he castigated Vigilantius for suggesting that the dead are impure: "Are the bishops of the whole world in error, who enter the basilicas of the dead, in which a 'worthless bit of dust and ashes lies wrapped up in a cloth, defiled and defiling all else?' Thus, according to you, the sacred buildings are like the sepulchers of the Pharisees, whitened without, while within they have filthy remains and are full of foul smells and uncleanness" (*Vigil.* 8).

Palestine had certainly changed a great deal since the early first century. Back then Jesus and his movement had tacitly agreed that tombs and the bones that they contained were ritually impure—the Torah said so, after all—but for Jerome, such boundaries were no longer operative. For him, the living and the dead could and should continue to have social contact, and such contact would not convey impurity of any kind. The dead were even welcome within the sacred space of the basilica. As such they now occupied a different social space than they had occupied in the world of Jesus. They had moved from the margin to the center.

Death ritual, as we have seen, does not change for light and transient causes. When Christians in Palestine during the early Byzantine period brought the bones of the dead from the margin into the center of the social world of the living, a number of long-term forces were at work, and one of the most powerful was the lasting influence of hellenization in Palestine. As Hellenism worked its way more thoroughly into the Jewish culture of Palestine during the second, third, and fourth centuries, it was a predictable result that some Jews would begin to make more extensive and substantial use of Greek and Roman death ritual. Hellenistic values had reached ever more deeply into the culture, touching with increasing force on more and more of the norms around which life was organized. The residential neighborhood on the western acropolis at Sepphoris clearly reflects this trend, with Hellenistic influences growing steadily stronger as the centuries pass. First-century homes, for example, were decorated with some Greek and Roman ornamentation, including frescoed walls, plaster moldings, and mosaic floors; but the floor plans of these houses were of traditional "courtyard" design, with historical roots in the so-called "four-roomed house" of early Israel. In addition, Jewish ritual baths (*miqva'ot*) and stone vessels give further indication of a strongly Jewish cultural context. By the third and fourth centuries, in contrast, Hellenistic elements had taken on a far greater prominence: the Greek "peristyle" floor plan had appeared, and mosaic floors featured pictorial representations. Over time, the cultural weight of Greece and Rome proved simply irresistible, and Jews eventually accommodated themselves to Hellenistic norms not only in their houses but also in their burial practices. All Jews were affected by the trend, and the bereaved soul who scrawled a familiar Hellenistic funerary epithet on the wall of Catacomb 12 at Beth She'arim was not untypical: "Be of good courage—no one is immortal."[10] Of all the Jewish groups in Palestine, however, it was the Christians who were in the best position not merely to accommodate themselves to Hellenistic norms but to take full advantage of the cultural trend, because Christian theological doctrines were so congenial to a cult of the dead. Jews, as we have seen, had long engaged in personal and private contact with the dead, but Christians held theological convictions that could easily make this private cult public. It would prove to be a relatively short step from the worship of the resurrected Christ to the full inclusion of the "dead in Christ" within the community of the living. Some Christian documents of the third and fourth centuries make the step explicit, by asserting that the "dead in Christ" are not really dead at all: "For they who have believed in God, according to the Gospel, even though they should sleep, they are not dead . . . for this cause therefore do you approach without restraint to those who are at rest, and hold them not unclean" (*Didas. Apost.* 6.22).

The cordial conjunction of Christian theological conviction with traditional Hellenistic norms regarding the dead made it possible for Christians to begin bringing the living and the dead together in the same social space, and the Christian cult of the dead can rightly be viewed as a development substantially rooted not only in Christian theology but also in traditional Hellenistic practices like *refrigeria* and *cenae novendiales*.

As Christians began to wed their claims about the resurrection of Jesus to traditional Hellenistic forms of death ritual during the third and fourth centuries, other changes were also appearing in the social structure of Palestine. Like those that had taken place earlier, as first Hellenism and then the Roman Empire arrived in Palestine from the West, these fresh changes were also the result of pressures from that direction. Historians have frequently noticed that as the fourth century wore on, many Roman cities (particularly in the East) began to feel social, financial, and political strains. In particular, the traditional system of urban architecture and finance, in which monumental public spaces were constructed through the generosity of prominent citizens, began to give way under its own weight. Growing numbers of wealthy citizens sought relief or escape from the increasingly burdensome obligations of public service, and construction and maintenance of public structures lagged. By the middle of the fourth century, especially in the East, "the transition from polis to medina—the gradual demise of the ancient city—was well underway."[11] In Palestine this trend showed itself at such sites as Beth She'an and Sepphoris in the decline of classical public structures: theaters, baths, colonnaded streets, and markets all fell into disrepair or were abandoned. At Beth She'an "the grandeur of the Roman urban planning deteriorated [and] the pragmatic Byzantine approach became more explicit."[12] At Sepphoris many of the stones from the theater (including perhaps the entire *scenae frons*) were stolen for use elsewhere, and the northern extent of the *cardo* was cut off by fresh construction. In place of traditional Roman monumental architecture there began to appear neighborhood enclaves and smaller industrial production facilities. The Roman city, in which all citizens participated in the public life of the polis, was giving way to the medina of the Arab period, in which social space would be parceled out in smaller clusters. It is not coincidental that distinctive forms of Christian death ritual began to appear at the same time as these broader social, political, and economic changes were reconfiguring the landscape of the ancient city. The pressures that undermined the unity of the city also had their impact on the cemetery. In the same way that it became possible to reconfigure the public space of the city, so also the cemetery could now be reconfigured along the lines of social groupings smaller than that of the classical polis. The cemetery, like the city, also became a medina. The death ritual of Early Byzantine Palestine thus has to do with a decomposing body—not merely a physical body that could be placed in an underground chamber for the dead, but also a social body that had once held Jews and Christians together in a shared culture, but that was now breaking down into its constituent parts.

The material culture of the early Byzantine period confirms that Christians in Palestine did begin to differentiate themselves from Jews in matters of death and burial during the fourth century. There are, for example, *arcosolium* tombs from this period that are decorated with crosses on the walls above the niches and on the lintels of the entrances. In one case a Greek cross was also incised into the surface of the stone that covered the entrance to a tomb.[13] In addition, many lead coffins from early Byzantine tombs evince characteristic methods of manufacture and patterns of decoration, but have Greek and/or Latin crosses along the short and long sides or *chi-rho* monograms on the lid.[14] Early Byzantine lamps inscribed with Greek crosses have also been found in the complex of tombs at Akeldama. These artifacts supply clear material evidence for the emergence of a distinctively Christian repertoire of funerary symbolism in the early Byzantine period. And this emerging Christian distinctiveness certainly did not stop with symbolism. By the fifth and sixth centuries, Christians in Palestine had brought the remains of corpses right into their church buildings, and performed "public worship in a proximity to the human dead which would have been profoundly disturbing to Jewish feeling."[15] Fifth-century Christian basilicas at Ein-Hanniya and Kafr Kama, for example, featured reliquaries set into the floor of their central apses, directly under the altar at the focal point of the sanctuary.[16] This "front and center" location was well-suited for use in the martyr cult, since the altar in the central apse was the focal point for the ritual of worship. Jerome, an enthusiastic supporter of such developments, asserted that since God is not the God of the dead but of the living, and "if the martyrs are alive" (*si ergo vivunt*), then they can and should have a place in gatherings for Christian worship (*Vigil. 5*). The social power of the Christian martyr cult issued, no doubt, from its liminality: like the *nulang* of the Berawan, these rituals brought participants into a marginal region along the boundary between life and death. By the fifth century, one could say that Jews and Christians in Palestine had come to approximate the Olo Ngaju and the Berawan in Borneo: one group forbade, while the other practiced, ritual contact between the dead and the living.

It has been said that "the early church tended to leapfrog the grave," suppressing the great sadness of human mortality with a "heady belief in the afterlife."[17] Perhaps, however, it would be more accurate to say instead that early Christians in Palestine *circumscribed* the grave, enclosing it—and the human corpse it contained—within an emerging vision of an ideal Christian society. In the early Byzantine period, the social structure of Palestine was changing dramatically, and contact with the dead, which had previously been personal and private, could now come out into the open. Drawing therefore upon energies that had long persisted below the surface of social life in Palestine, Christians transformed a secret Jewish cult of the dead into an open Christian one. Explicitly denying the impurity of corpses, they began to do in public what had previously been done only in private, and to do on a large scale what had earlier been done only on a small scale. In particular, by going public with their cult of the dead, Christians re-inscribed the circumference of the social order, moving the dead from a position of marginality and exclusion to a location at or near the social center. Public gatherings in the tombs became common, and portions of dead bodies were brought into the center of places of religious worship, where they became the focal point of public ritual and ceremony. The Christian dead had become, as Greek and Roman dead had been for some time, valued members of the social network.

In a series of articles concerned with persistence and change in Mediterranean religions, Jonathan Z. Smith has argued for the presence in late antiquity of two distinctive religious world views, the "locative" and the "utopian."[18] Citing examples as far back as the Gilgamesh epic, Smith argues that "locative" traditions are oriented essentially toward the creation and preservation of order, and toward the establishment and maintenance of boundaries. The soteriology of these religious world views emphasizes emplacement, cleansing, sanctification, and rectification. In the face of death, such religions offer their adherents a symbolic system through which the inevitability of death can be accepted, tolerated, and even celebrated. As Smith puts it, "in locative traditions, what is soteriological is for the dead to remain dead."[19] Early Judaism in Roman Palestine was certainly a "locative" religious world view, and so was early Christianity, at least until the beginning of the fourth century. There is evidence to indicate that at that point in time Christianity began to move toward as a "utopian" religious world view. Smith has argued, in fact, that the fourth century saw the reinterpretation of several "locative" Mediterranean religions in a "utopian" direction. "Utopian" traditions, he maintains, are oriented not toward sanctification and emplacement, but toward "salvation achieved through acts of rebellion and transcendence."[20] In the face of death, they supply their followers with symbolic resources for believing that death is neither inevitable nor final.

The dying and rising of a god is often a conspicuous feature of such traditions, of which the Hellenistic mysteries supply several examples. The emergence of the early Christian martyr cult in early Byzantine Palestine might be another example of a "locative" Mediterranean religious world view "straining in a utopian direction."[21] There are good reasons to regard the emergence of the early Christian martyr cult in Palestine as a particular example of this general phenomenon. In this regard it is especially significant that some of the texts associated with the early Christian martyr cult in Palestine do explicitly assert that death has been or can be transcended. Both Jerome and the *Didascalia Apostolorum*, for example, justify the martyr cult with the straightforward declaration that Christian dead are not really dead but alive. On this basis they deny that the dead have to be separated from the social network of the living. This assertion about transcendence over death, warranted by Christian theological affirmations about the resurrection of Christ, marks the early Christian martyr cult as an example of Smith's category of "utopian" religious tradition. One of the most problematic exigencies of the human condition—mortality—is suppressed by a heady assertion of resurrection.

Perhaps there is a sense, however, in which the early Christian martyr cult is still "locative," in Smith's sense of that term. If "locative" religious traditions offer their adherents security, stability, and rectification through the correct emplacement and ordering of life, then the martyr cult does continue to have certain "locative" aspects. For with this cult, the dead, who were formerly situated beyond the margins of the social network, are firmly relocated to a position in the center of public life. Beneath the altar in the central apse at the front of the church sanctuary was in fact as central a location as the early church could provide, and it became the place in which one could find the living dead in Christ. On this basis we might describe the early Christian martyr cult in Palestine as both "utopian" (since it offered its adherents transcendence over death) and "re-locative," since it re-situated and re-emplaced the dead in a new and different (and more prominent) social location. Brought from the margin to the center, the dead could now communicate power and sanctification, rather than impurity and danger.

The fact that early Christians began to see such possibilities during the fourth century marks that period as an important moment in the story of the birth of Judaism and Christianity.

Notes to Chapter 4

1. Typical examples include S. van Tilborg, *The Jewish Leaders in Matthew* (Leiden: Brill, 1972); D. R. A. Hare, *The Theme of Jewish Persecution of Christians in the Gospel According to St. Matthew* (Cambridge: Cambridge University Press, 1967); J. L. Martyn, *History and Theology in the Fourth Gospel* (New York: Harper & Row, 1968).

2. Again, typical examples include F. V. Filson, *A New Testament History* (Philadelphia: Westminster, 1964), 331; L. Goppelt, *Jesus, Paul, and Judaism: An Introduction to New Testament Theology* (trans. E. Schroeder; New York: Nelson, 1964), 129; B. Reicke, *Neutestamentliche Zeitgeschichte: die biblische Welt 500 v.–100 n.Chr.* (Berlin: Topelmann, 1965), 157.

3. The metaphor of "fraternal twins" is from Alan Segal; cf. A. Segal, *Rebecca's Children: Judaism and Christianity in the Roman World* (Cambridge, Mass.: Harvard University Press, 1986), 179. Before Segal, Marcel Simon had already described Judaism and Christianity as "brothers"; cf. M. Simon, *Verus Israel: A Study of the Relations between Christians and Jews in the Roman Empire (135–425)* (trans. H. McKeating; Oxford: Oxford University Press, 1986), xiii.

4. D. Boyarin, *Dying for God: Martyrdom and the Making of Christianity and Judaism* (Stanford: Stanford University Press, 1999), 5.

5. To be sure, the Franciscan archaeologists Bellarmino Bagatti and Emmanuelle Testa did attempt to produce funerary evidence in support of their argument for an early emergence of distinctive Christianity in Palestine, but their claims, which were never widely accepted, were convincingly answered by Joan Taylor. Cf. B. Bagatti, *The Church from the Circumcision* (trans. E. Hoade; Jerusalem: Franciscan, 1971); E. Testa, *Il Simbolismo dei Giudeo-Cristiani* (Jerusalem: Franciscan, 1969); and J. Taylor, *Christians and the Holy Places: The Myth of Jewish-Christian Origins* (Oxford: Clarendon, 1993).

6. Byron R. McCane, "Let the Dead Bury Their Own Dead: Secondary Burial and Mt. 8:21–22," *Harvard Theological Review* 83 (1990): 31–43.

7. D. Boyarin, *Dying for God*, title of the introduction.

8. A. F. J. Klijn, "The Study of Jewish Christianity," *New Testament Studies* 20 (1973): 430.

9. A. Marmorstein, "Judaism and Christianity in the Middle of the Third Century," *Hebrew Union College Annual* 10 (1935): 240.

10. N. Avigad, *Catacombs 12–23* (vol. 3 of *Beth She'arim*; New Brunswick: Rutgers University Press, 1971), 26.

11. C. Thomas McCollough, "Monumental Changes: Architecture and Culture in Late Roman and Byzantine Sepphoris" (paper presented at the Annual Meeting of ASOR/SE, March 1999). I am grateful to Professor McCollough for a copy of this paper.

12. G. Foerster and Y. Tsafrir, "From Scythopolis to Baysan," in *The Byzantine and Early Islamic Near East, Vol. II.* (eds. A Cameron and L. Conrad; Princeton: Darwin Press, 1992), 105.

13. W. J. Moulton, "A Painted Christian Tomb at Beit Jibrin," *Annual of the American Schools of Oriental Research* 2–3 (1921–22): 95-102, pl. 1–5.

14. M. Avi-Yonah, "Lead Coffins from Palestine I," *Quarterly of the Department of Antiquities in Palestine* 4 (1935): 87–99. Idem, "Lead Coffins from Palestine II," *Quarterly of the Department of Antiquities in Palestine* 4 (1935): 138–53. L. Y. Rahmani, "On Some Recently Discovered Lead Coffins from Israel," *Israel Exploration Journal* 36 (1986): 234–50. Idem, "More Lead Coffins from Israel," *Israel Exploration Journal* 37 (1987): 123–46.

15. P. Brown, *The Cult of the Saints* (Chicago: University of Chicago Press, 1981), 9.

16. D. C. Baramki, "An Early Christian Reliquary at 'Ein-Hanniya," *Quarterly of the Department of Antiquities in Palestine* 3 (1933): 113–17. A. Saarisalo, "Kafr Kama," *Israel Exploration Journal* 13 (1963): 149–50.

17. Brown, *The Cult of the Saints*, 70.

18. J. Z. Smith, *Drudgery Divine: On the Comparison of Early Christianities and the Religions of Late Antiquity* (Chicago: University of Chicago Press, 1990), 121.

19. Ibid., 124.

20. Ibid., 133.

21. Ibid., 133.

Rest in Peace or Roast in Hell:
Funerary versus Apocalyptic
Portraits of Paradise

The preceding chapters have shown that distinctively Christian death ritual did not emerge in Palestine before the fourth century, and that it was made possible at that time by changes in the social structure. The slow but steady breakdown of social institutions that had supported the Hellenistic city opened up a public space into which early Christianity's cult of the dead was able to emerge. In this cult the circumference of the social network was re-inscribed along overtly Christian lines, offering a vision of an ideal Christian society re-centered around the dead, who were brought from a marginal place of impurity to a central position of prominence and power. As the Hellenistic city broke down into its constituent parts, this Christian social network became one of the neighborhoods into which individuals were able to re-situate themselves, their families, their lives, and their deaths. Despite the decline of the Hellenistic city, however, traditional Greek norms were still exerting substantial influence. The Christian cult of the dead gave public expression to practices that had persisted in private for centuries, and its emergence in Palestine was one aspect of the long encounter between Judaism and Hellenism. In this chapter I would like to look briefly at one final example of this encounter. In what follows I would like to make the case that late ancient Christian constructs of the afterlife were also significantly shaped by both Hellenistic and Jewish portraits of paradise.

Consider the following two late ancient portraits of paradise. The first is engraved on a *loculus* niche covering from Ostia, probably from the late second or early third century C.E. It is a picture of a meal, with the deceased reclining alongside his wife on a couch, while attendants on either side bring baskets laden with food. Two winged creatures flank the scene on the far right and the far left, and what appears to be either a small dog or puppy looks on from beneath the couch. Even at first glance it is clear that this is a portrait of a domestic scene, with dominant themes of rest, well-being, and contentment, as the living and the dead continuing to enjoy each other's company.[1] The second portrait is contained in the following excerpt from the *Apocalypse of Paul*:

> And when I had entered into the gates of Paradise there came to meet me Enoch, whose face shone as the sun. And he embraced me and said: "Hail, Paul, dearly beloved of God." And with joyful face he kissed me. And then he began to weep. And I said to him: "Father, why are you weeping?" And he sighed and wept again, and said: "Because we are injured by humans and they trouble us much; for there are many good things which the Lord has prepared, but many do not accept them." And I entered within that place and immediately I saw Elijah and he came and greeted me with gladness and joy. And when he had seen me, he turned away and wept and said to me, "Paul, may you receive the reward for the work which you have accomplished among humankind. As for me, I have seen the great and numerous good things which God has prepared for all the righteous, but the majority do not accept them." (*Apoc. Paul* 20)[2]

What a different impression this portrait makes. Here the scene is not domestic but heavenly, and there is no meal, nor any emphasis on peace, well-being, or rest: on the contrary, it appears that virtually everyone in paradise is on the verge of breaking down in tears.

Among the many reasons for the differences between these portraits of paradise, one of the most important is that they come from different social settings. The first portrait is *funerary*: it is the decoration on a stone cover from a burial niche, and to see it, one would have had to enter the catacombs of the dead. The second portrait, by contrast, is *apocalyptic*: it is the vision of an early Christian group in which ideas of final judgment were vibrant, and to see this portrait one would have had to participate in such a group. Differences in their social contexts cause funerary and apocalyptic portraits of paradise to diverge in characteristic ways.

In their social context, apocalyptic portraits (like the *Apocalypse of Paul*) are theodicies: they respond to the problem of evil, and ultimately to the inevitability of human death. They evoke a picture of a place and time when death will not have the last word. They unfurl over the heads of those who face the certainty of death a banner, richly embroidered with a picture of paradise, and under that banner mortal souls can march a little more confidently toward their inescapable fate.[3] But in their social context, funerary portraits of paradise (like the *loculus* niche cover) are dirges of mourning: they respond not to the certainty of an eventual death but to the reality of a recent one. They soften the fresh impact of death with a glimpse through the veil to the other side. They apply to the wounds of those whose lives have been torn by death a balm, richly oiled with a picture of paradise, and soothed by that balm mortal souls can find their way to personal and social healing. Both types of portrait belong to the equipment by which early Christianity fought its battle against death, but in late antiquity each had its own distinctive social location and its own particular religious content. As a result, neither was mixed with the other: in late antiquity, apocalyptic portraits of paradise did not appear in funerary contexts because the wounded could not be expected to carry their army's flag into battle.

Funerary portraits of paradise are relatively rare; most ancient funerary art depicts not visions of paradise but images of the good life here on Earth. Those portraits of paradise that do appear, however, typically employ a standard vocabulary of symbols in order to emphasize broadly comforting themes of rest, well-being, peace, and reunion. The figures in the Ostia *loculus* niche cover, for example, are arranged in almost perfect symmetrical balance, and the naked upper body of the deceased recalls the conventions of heroic sculpture from the Hellenistic period. Scenes of this type, known as *klinē* reliefs because of the couch at the center, are frequent in sarcophagus reliefs from the second and third centuries. Typically they include some or all of the following elements: the deceased reclines on a couch in the center of the piece, sometimes with the spouse; figures on the right or left (or both) carry baskets of food; a particularly common image is that of a female figure just to the left of the deceased, seated in a chair made from woven material, strumming a stringed instrument; a three-legged table covered with fish frequently sits near the couch, and a dog or puppy is often to be found beneath or in front of it. Interpretation of these reliefs has repeatedly run aground on the vexed question of whether they represent recollections of life on Earth, or anticipations of joys in the afterlife. Himmelmann has tried to resolve this difficulty by proposing that *klinē* reliefs are allegorical representations of early Greek meals with the dead, but one must wonder why he felt it necessary to insert the word "allegorical." For as we saw in the introduction, antiquity was a time in which many people believed that one could indeed dine with the dead, and there was a specific kind of meal that belonged both to the customary experiences of mortal life on Earth and to the anticipated joys of the afterlife. I refer of course to the *refrigerium*, that "refreshing" meal eaten at the tomb or graveside on specific regular ritual occasions when the dead were commemorated. In Roman society, for example, the *cena novendialis* was a graveside feast held on the ninth day after death, and the annual observance of the *Parentalia* each February also involved ritual dining with the dead at the tomb or grave. In addition, graveside feasts on the anniversary of a loved one's death had been customary as far back as the Roman Republic. The dead were certainly believed to participate in such meals. Lucian reports that wine was poured out for them (*Luct.* 9), often into tubes driven into the ground for that purpose, and trays in the shapes of particular foods were carved into the *mensae* that covered many graves. Sophisticates like Lucian might not have approved—for that matter neither did Christian bishops like Ambrose and Augustine— but at these meals the living and the dead were believed to dine together. Thus it is no coincidence that *klinē* reliefs depict it just that way, with the deceased right in the center of the scene.

Closely related to, but chronologically later than the *klinē* reliefs are sarcophagus reliefs and catacomb paintings that depict the so-called *stibadium* or sigma meal. In these portraits from the late third and early fourth centuries C.E., the dominant themes are once again well-being, abundance, and togetherness. A group of five to seven people is seated together around a semi-circular table or bolster, with food and drink laid out generously before them. Often the three-legged table of fish reappears. Unlike the *klinē* reliefs, however, none of the figures in these *stibadium* scenes occupies a clearly marked place of greatest importance, and none is easily identifiable as the deceased. No winged figures frame the scene, and the meal sometimes appears to be taking place outdoors. On the whole, the style is more realistic than idealistic. For these reasons Himmelmann has argued that *stibadium* scenes should be interpreted as idyllic representations, similar to those of hunting and harvesting that are so frequent on sarcophagi.[4] Certainly it is true that late ancient funerary art often included depictions of abundance in earthly life, and hunting and harvest scenes symbolically represented much of what the Roman upper classes thought was best about human existence. Yet during the late Roman Empire the *stibadium* seating arrangement also became increasingly popular for both indoor and outdoor banquets, including graveside *refrigeria*, which naturally took place out of doors. In addition, Robin Jensen has shown that while pagans may have employed this motif as an idyllic symbol, by as early as the third century Christians in some regions of the empire were already adapting it as a portrait of paradise.[5] In view of these considerations it is likely that when *stibadium* scenes occur in funerary contexts, they are representations of meals with the dead.

Images like these were powerful because they spoke directly to the acute problems that death posed for the social system of late antiquity. The symbolic force of meals with the dead caused even Christians to make use of these images—a *klinē* relief appears on the lid of the sarcophagus of Junius Bassus. We know that Jews too were drawn into the practice of dining with the dead, since cooking pots are one of the most common finds in Jewish tombs from Roman Palestine. For even though philosophers and religious leaders may have taught that one should remain tranquil in the face of death, over and over again in our sources we can read expressions of what really bothered the ancients about it: their dread of loss. The worst thing about death was what it did to survivors, those who had to live on without those who had been taken away. After losing his wife and two sons, Quintilian lamented that "I live on, and must find a reason to live on" (*Inst.* 6.14), and Pliny the Younger once wrote that he sometimes felt as if he could still see and hear and touch his deceased mentor Verginius Rufus (*Ep.* 2.1.12). The Babylonian Talmud tells the story of Rabban Gamaliel's profound grief at the death of his servant Tebbi who was "like a righteous one" (*'Ebel RabbatI* 1b), and more than one funerary inscription laments the unexpected loss of a spouse, friend, or relative. A first-century epitaph from Leontopolis (*Corpus inscriptionum judaicarum* 1511), for example, invites passersby to "weep all together for the one who has suddenly gone."

From this perspective we can begin to understand why funerary portraits of paradise tend to present pictures of meals with the dead, for in so doing they ameliorated the psychological and social experience of loss. These portraits of paradise served to create a symbolic setting in which the blow of separation could be lifted, if only momentarily. The wounds inflicted by death were soothed by a picture, a picture in which the opacity of separation was rendered temporarily translucent. Recall, especially, that these portraits appear on the sides and lids of sarcophagi, the covers of burial niches, and on the walls of catacombs. They are, in other words, the realia of funeral ceremony, the material detritus of death ritual. In antiquity one would have seen these portraits only at specific and particular moments during the ritual process of death: at the time of interment, on the ninth day after death, on the anniversary of death, or during the *Parentalia*. Further, the ancients would have viewed these funerary portraits of paradise only in a specific location, namely, in a tomb or catacomb. To see these reliefs and paintings, one would have had to enter the realm of the dead and go down into those spaces reserved for them. Pictures of meals with the dead, in other words, did their work of symbolic representation in the immediate physical context of death and the dead, at times and places where the senses would already have been saturated with unrelenting evidence of human mortality. With their couches, tables, and food, their puppy dogs and strumming women, these portraits silently but persuasively addressed a grim reality. They were balm for the wound of loss, healing for the psychological experience of grief.

There were social and cultural dimensions to funerary portraits of paradise as well. Socially, they supported the function of death ritual as a rite of passage. As Arnold van Gennep and many others have observed, death ritual is a ceremonial process that supervises the transition of a member of society from the world of the living to the world of the dead.[6] In late antiquity, *klinē* reliefs and *stibadium* scenes facilitated this ritual function by symbolically signifying the passage of the deceased into a new location in the social system, specifically a location among the dead with whom one could (occasionally) dine. Social transactions made necessary by death—reallocation of the deceased's material property and sexual partner, for example—were aided and abetted by symbolic images that depicted the deceased as happily situated in his or her new social location. It should also be noted that these portraits were an upper-class phenomenon, enjoyed primarily by those who had the means to pay for their creation. Members of the lower classes may have imagined the presence of their departed loved one at a funerary banquet, but they could not afford to create a material picture of it. Portraits of meals with the dead are also culturally significant, for they reflect an effort to fight off the despair of death through symbolic representations of life and abundance. Drawing upon ideals whose deepest roots were in early Greece, *klinē* reliefs and *stibadium* scenes used a portrait of paradise—replete with food, music, and loved ones—in order to tilt the balance of power back in favor of life.

Like funerary portraits of paradise, apocalyptic portraits of paradise are also relatively rare. Apocalypticists were, on the whole, a good deal more interested in hell than in heaven, and tours of hell are much more frequent than portraits of paradise.[7] At times, however, we do find depictions of a blessed afterlife, such as in the *Apocalypse of Paul*, "one of the most popular apocalypses in the early church."[8] This document, written in Greek during the fourth century, imaginatively reconstructs what Paul supposedly saw when he was "caught up into the third heaven" (2 Cor 12:2), and it seems that no one up there was dining with the dead. Instead, Paul is said to have beheld sights that turn out to be rather typical of late ancient apocalyptic portraits of paradise. There were, for example, angels keeping track of all the deeds done by everyone on Earth each day and reporting those deeds to God each evening. Paul also saw that at the moment of death, every human soul is escorted by an angel to the presence of God for judgment (*Apoc. Paul* 7, 16). Not surprisingly, this motif of judgment runs rather consistently through other apocalyptic depictions of the afterlife as well. In the *Martyrdom and Ascension of Isaiah*, Isaiah sees the books in which are written all the deeds done by everyone on Earth, and in the *Apocalypse of Peter*, Jesus describes in excruciating detail the events that will unfold "on the day of the decision of the judgement of God" (*Apoc. Pet.* 4). *1 Enoch* 25 (the Book of the Watchers) describes "the throne, where the Holy and Great One . . . will sit" for judgment, and *1 Enoch* 69 (the Similitudes) foresees the day when "the Son of Man will sit on the throne of his glory." The *Testament of Levi*'s portrait of paradise is quite brief, but not too brief to mention that "the Lord will execute judgment on humanity" (*Test. Levi* 4). Even pagan views of the afterlife could be shaped by ideas of punishment and reward: in Book 6 of the *Aeneid,* Virgil takes his hero into an underworld where the shades in death are separated on the basis of their character and conduct in life.

Perhaps here we can begin to understand the weeping that so dominated our first look at paradise in the *Apocalypse of Paul.* Since these portraits emphasize the certainty of future judgment, they do not bring good news for all. Everyone will someday get exactly what he or she deserves, and thus some will have to be punished. Indeed, according to the *Apocalypse of Paul,* most of humankind will miss out on the rewards of paradise. As a tearful Elijah puts it, "The promises of God are great, but the majority do not accept them, and only with difficulty through many labors do a few enter into these places" (*Apoc. Paul* 20). These depictions of tears in heaven, then, offer symbolic reinforcement to the Christian assertion that a day of reckoning lies ahead. Through a portrait of paradise that transcends the limits of time and space, readers are reassured that Christian declarations about judgment day are true and will someday ultimately come to pass. Such claims were evidently in need of support during late antiquity—at least within the groups wherein apocalyptic literature circulated—for in this period Christian apocalypses increasingly turned away from depictions of the antichrist (the Book of Revelation, for example) toward more and more vivid reports of "heaven and its blessedness, and hell and its miseries."[9] Readers of documents such as the *Apocalypse of Paul* felt themselves to be in a minority in a world that appeared to be taking little note of them, and symbolic representations of tears in heaven helped to belay the rising sense of anomie that clearly accompanied their experience of inferior status.

In keeping with the motif of judgment, apocalyptic portraits of paradise also often depict heaven as a place of different regions and levels, representing the afterlife as a sort of spiritual meritocracy stratified by righteousness. Paul, for example, is caught up to the third heaven, but Isaiah is transported all the way up to the seventh heaven, where he beholds "all the righteous from the time of Adam onwards" (*Mart. Ascen. Isa.* 9.7), along with robes and thrones prepared for those yet to come. In the *Apocalypse of Paul* the stratification of rewards is related to very specific behaviors. Paul's tour of "the city of Christ"—a region of the second heaven reserved for "those who have not sinned"—includes visions of the rewards prepared for those who have kept their marriages pure (*Apoc. Paul* 22), given hospitality to strangers (27), and those unlearned souls who "neither knew the Scriptures nor many Psalms but paid heed to one chapter and . . . acted with carefulness in conformity" to it (29). Sometimes the rewards presuppose a very specific social setting. Outside the gates of the city of Christ, for example, Paul saw the souls of those whose eternal fate was the direct result of their behavior within the community of a monastery: "These are those who fasting day and night have zealously practiced renunciation, but they have had a heart proud beyond that of other men in that they have glorified and praised themselves and done nothing for their neighbors. For some they greeted in a friendly way, but to others they did not even say 'Greetings': and to whom they wished they opened the doors of the monastery, and if they did some small good to their neighbor they became puffed up" (24).

One final characteristic of apocalyptic portraits of paradise is also of interest for our purposes: in these documents, heaven is described in grand and extravagant terms. In Rev 21, for example, John measures the boundaries of the new Jerusalem and finds that the city is 12,000 stadia (or about 1,400 miles) on each side, dimensions that "struggle to express in symbols the vastness and splendor"[10] of the city. Isaiah, upon seeing Christ and the Holy Spirit in the seventh heaven, is overwhelmed by the "great power" and "great glory" that emanate from them (*Asc. Isa.* 9.27–42). And Paul finds the "land of promise" to be a place of extraordinary abundance, bounty, and productivity. There are rivers flowing with milk and honey, and fruit trees and vines that bloom twelve times a year, each cluster producing ten thousand dates or grapes (*Apoc. Paul* 22).

Inevitable judgment, stratified levels of reward, eschatological abundance—with such themes apocalyptic portraits of paradise addressed chronic inequities in the social structure of late antiquity.

The people who wrote, read, heard, and preserved these portraits regarded their world as a place of relative deprivation in which they felt themselves unfairly disadvantaged.[11] The details vary from place to place and from group to group, but in late antiquity apocalyptic was, as a rule, an ideology for the disprivileged, an antidote to the felt experience of powerlessness, anonymity, and vulnerability. Paul's visit to the gate of paradise (*Apoc. Paul* 19) poignantly captures this aspect of the genre. As he approaches the gate, Paul looks up and notices that above it are two golden tablets covered with letters.

> And I asked the angel and said: Sir, tell me, for what reason are these letters set on those tables? The angel answered and said to me: These are the names of the righteous who while they dwell on earth serve God with a whole heart. And again I said: Are then their names written in heaven while they are still on earth? And he said: Not only their names but also their faces are written, and the likeness of those who serve God is in heaven, and the servants of God, who serve him with a whole heart, are known to the angels before they leave the world. (*Apoc. Paul* 19)

Christians who served Christ with a whole heart might indeed experience anonymity and insignificance in society, and even within the monastery there might have been doors that were closed to them, but in an apocalyptic portrait of paradise they would find reassurance that the highest powers in the universe were already taking notice of them.

Apocalyptic portraits of paradise were therefore a form of theodicy, offering their readers an explanation of how it could be that the wicked prosper here on Earth while the righteous go unrewarded. Yet it would be a mistake to conclude that these portraits are principally a symbolic expression of lower-class resentment.[12] Not only would that view oversimplify social relations in late antiquity—in which terms such as "lower class" and "middle class" are not always useful—but it would also overlook the fact that these apocalyptic portraits of paradise are pictures of the *afterlife*. They address themselves not merely to vague and anxious feelings of anomie and disprivilege, but rather to specific fears caused by the all-too-human certainty of death. They portray a paradise in which the just are properly rewarded *after death*. As such, apocalyptic portraits of paradise evoke images of transcendence in order to mount a symbolic protest against the possibility that death might bring merely an end, rather than a resolution. By looking beyond the boundary of death, they hold out the promise that even a mortal life of disprivilege can have meaning and value. Even those who "neither knew the Scriptures nor many Psalms but paid heed to one chapter" can know that their names are inscribed on the gates of heaven.

As was the case with funerary portraits of paradise, one had to enter a specific social setting in order to view these apocalyptic pictures of heaven. No doubt the present text of our *Apocalypse of Paul* reached its current form within the confines of a monastery. Other apocalypses certainly circulated among Christian groups whose members lacked significant wealth, status, power, or prestige. Unlike the funerary portraits of paradise, then, which came from the burial places of the upper classes and which were associated with specific funerary rituals, these apocalyptic pictures of the afterlife appear to have originated in the daily social life of religious conventicles and minority groups, which did not likely include members of the upper classes.

By this point it should be clear, however, that apocalyptic and funerary portraits of paradise do have one significant characteristic in common, and it is a characteristic that goes to the heart of their religious and social power. Both alike are replete with symbols of abundance. From baskets overflowing with bread, to tables covered with fish, from vines that produce twelve times annually, to cities that stretch the limits of comprehension, these visions of paradise mount a sustained symbolic assault on scarcity, want, and deprivation. They overwhelm death with symbols of life, burying human mortality beneath a symbolic cascade of heavenly plenty. Therein lies their essential unity, for both apocalyptic and funerary portraits of paradise are projections of the human refusal to give death the last word. For some time now human beings, individually and collectively, have been waging war against a force that threatens to engulf all that means anything to us, fighting to protect ourselves and those we love from the apparently inexorable consuming power of death. In late antiquity, portraits of paradise were a weapon of choice.

Yet these two kinds of portrait certainly reflect two different moments in the conflict between humans and death. Apocalyptic visions come, as it were, from the center of the battlefield, where combat is joined and where, in the confusion of war, it is not always entirely clear which side has the upper hand. The social circles in which these portraits flourished were contending with chronic experiences of anomie, disprivilege, and relative deprivation. Apocalyptic portraits of paradise mount a counterattack against the nagging fear that at the end of the day, human life may not ultimately make any sense. Perhaps in fact apocalyptic portraits do seem strangely haunted by the uneasy suspicion that death may be getting the better of the struggle, for our sources betray a slightly overeager inclination to rally the troops with promises of reinforcements from the highest levels of heaven. The picture of Enoch and Elijah weeping by the gates of paradise seems just a little overdone. Funerary portraits, by contrast, come from the field hospital, where triage is administered to those who have been overwhelmed and injured by the foe. The social circles in which these portraits circulated were wealthy and privileged, and thus not afflicted by chronic anomie; yet such persons could still be (and regularly were) acutely wounded by grief and loss. Even the well-to-do had to face the social dislocations caused by the death of one of their own. And here, it seems to me, we have come upon the principal reason why during late antiquity apocalyptic depictions of paradise tended not to appear in funerary contexts. The social energies that produced an apocalypse (anonymity and disprivilege) were so different from those that inspired funerary symbolism (dislocation and grief), that a combination of the two—that is, an apocalyptic sarcophagus relief—would have been as out of place as a bugler in an intensive care unit.[13]

Of course the time would eventually come when apocalyptic ideology would circulate not merely among the disenfranchised but also in the centers of power. In medieval Christianity, apocalyptic symbolism would become a potent tool used by ecclesiastical elites to enforce conformity and submission to authority. But not in late antiquity. In our time period, as the sarcophagus of Junius Bassus so clearly indicates, even those who believed that the Son of Man would one day judge the world still softened the blow of grief by picturing a meal with their dear departed.

NOTES TO CHAPTER 5

1. N. Himmelmann, *Typologische Untersuchungen an Römischen Sarkophagreliefs des 3. und 4. Jahrhunderts n. Chr.* (Mainz: Philipp von Zabern, 1973), 18.

2. Unless otherwise noted, English translations of apocalyptic documents in this chapter are taken from M. G. Reddish, ed., *Apocalyptic Literature: A Reader* (Peabody, Mass.: Hendrickson, 1995).

3. Peter Berger, *The Sacred Canopy* (Garden City, N.Y.: Doubleday, 1967), 52.

4. Himmelmann, *Typologische*, 25–26.

5. Robin A. Jensen, "Dining in Paradise," *Bible Review* (October 1998): 32–49.

6. Van Gennep, *The Rites of Passage.*

7. Himmelfarb, *Tours of Hell.*

8. Reddish, *Apocalyptic Literature*, 291.

9. P. Vielhauer, "Apocalyptic," in *New Testament Apocrypha, Vol. 2.* (eds. E. Hennecke and W. Schneemelcher; trans. R. McL. Wilson; Philadelphia: Westminster, 1965), 600.

10. I. T. Beckwith, *The Apocalypse of John* (Grand Rapids: Baker, 1979), 760.

11. John G. Gager, *Kingdom and Community: The Social World of Early Christianity* (Engelwood Cliffs, N.J.: Prentice Hall, 1975), 27. Cf. also Adela Y. Collins, *Crisis and Catharsis: The Power of the Apocalypse* (Philadelphia: Westminster, 1984), 84–110.

12. Max Weber, *The Sociology of Religion* (trans. E. Fischoff; Boston: Beacon, 1991), 110–17.

13. At first glance it might seem that 1 Thess 4:13–18 forms an exception to this assertion, since both funerary and apocalyptic content appear to be present in that text, but as a matter of fact the subject matter is entirely apocalyptic. The problem of "those who have fallen asleep" is not caused by the pain of grief in a funerary social context, but by a difficulty of theology in an apocalyptic social context. The issue in the community at Thessalonica is not that people are grieving, but that they are confronted by a theological dilemma inherent in apocalyptic eschatology. Specifically, will those who survive to the End have an advantage over those who do not? In the stratification of apocalyptic rewards, will survivors find themselves on a higher level than "those who have fallen asleep?" As A. F. J. Klijn has shown, this question is known in other apocalyptic documents from early Judaism and Christianity, especially 4 Ezra: "1 Thess. 4:13–18 can be explained entirely against the background of apocalyptic thinking. That applies to the question asked and the answer given. The question arose from the emphasis laid upon the end of time and the fate of those arriving at this end. . . . The unanimous answer was that at the

end all people involved would partake in the events at the same time. . . . Paul's answer was traditional. It is the answer of the apocalypses." A. F. J. Klijn, "1 Thessalonians 4:13–18 and Its Background," in *Paul and Paulinism: Essays in honour of C. K. Barrett* (eds. M. D. Hooker and S. G. Wilson; London: SPCK, 1982), 72.

Conclusion:
James, son of Joseph, brother of Jesus

In late October 2002, news media around the world enthusiastically reported the announcement of an archaeological discovery of extraordinary significance. According to reliable sources, "the earliest known documentation of Jesus outside the Bible" had surfaced in Jerusalem.[1] A plain and undecorated ossuary, previously kept in the private holdings of an amateur collector of antiquities, had been found to bear an inscription reading (in Aramaic): "Ya`acob bar Yosef ahui diYeshua," or "James, son of Joseph, brother of Jesus." The eminent French epigrapher André Lemaire declared in the pages of the magazine *Biblical Archaeology Review* that "it seems very probable that this is the ossuary of the James in the New Testament. If so, this would also mean that we have here the first epigraphic mention—from about 63 C.E.—of Jesus of Nazareth."[2] Lemaire's claim was immediately met with skeptical responses from archaeologists. Several agreed that the ossuary was interesting and potentially significant, but all expressed concern that it had come to light from a private collection rather than through a controlled archaeological excavation. Since its archaeological context was unknown, these archaeologists observed, its authenticity could never be positively confirmed. In subsequent news reports during the early weeks of November, further questions came to light regarding the circumstances under which the artifact had surfaced. The time, place, and method of its acquisition through the antiquities market all became matters of uncertainty, leading one prominent archaeologist to remark, "To say the least, I have a very bad feeling about the matter."[3] Clearly there are good reasons to be circumspect in our appraisal and interpretation of this artifact. Amid the welter of competing claims and possibilities, however, one point is assured: the practice of Jewish and Christian death ritual in Early Roman Palestine, which has been examined in these pages, provides the appropriate historical context within which to assess its significance.

The "burial box of James" (as *BAR* called it) has all the characteristics of a typical Jewish ossuary from the Early Roman period. It was formed from a block of the soft limestone chalk which is so plentiful in the geology of Jerusalem. Testing by the Geological Survey of the Ministry of National Infrastructures of Israel identified the likely source of the stone as an ancient limestone quarry in the area of Mt. Scopus in Jerusalem. With dimensions of 50.5 x 25 x 30.5 cm (20 x 10 x 12 inches), the ossuary is within the range of ossuary sizes commonly used for the reburial of bones of adults. Like most Jewish ossuaries from this period, this one is roughly and unevenly hewn. One of the short sides, for example, is not quite perpendicular to the base, giving the ossuary a slightly trapezoidal shape. Chisel marks and scratches are plainly evident across all its surfaces. The lid is nearly flat, very slightly convex, and the bottom is flat, with no feet. It shows signs of an attempt at decoration. Each face (including the lid) is framed by a thinly incised straight line running along the outside edge, 1.2 cm (0.5 inches) from the edge, and on one long side (opposite the inscription) are the preliminary marks used by carvers for creating the rosettes which are so common on Jewish ossuaries in early Roman Jerusalem. All of these features are well-known among Jewish ossuaries from the Early Roman period in Jerusalem.

An inscription, incised with a nail or other sharp object, runs across the middle of the right half of one of the long sides. Made up of twenty Aramaic letters, the inscription is 19.5cm (7.5 inches) long and 0.9 cm (0.33 inches) high. The script is neatly rendered, with no spaces between the words, and the reading is clearly legible, with no letters uncertain: "Ya`acob bar Yosef ahui diYeshua," or "James, son of Joseph, brother of Jesus." The form and content of the inscription are, like the other features of this ossuary, typical of the Early Roman period in Jerusalem. The script includes some of the common variations in the ancient spellings of names like James, Joseph, and Jesus. "Ya`acob," for example, which was sometimes written with and sometimes without the letter *waw*, is written with the *waw*. "Yosef," which could be written with or without the letter *he* ("Yehosef"), is written without the *he*. "Yeshua" is a common variation in the spelling of a name which could also be rendered "Yehoshua" or "Yeshu." The script includes both cursive and formal lettering, with cursive forms of *aleph, daleth,* and *yod* in the words "ahui diYeshua." A few observers have speculated that the presence of these cursive forms might indicate that this closing phrase was added later by a second hand, perhaps even by a modern forger. Lemaire correctly notes, however, that the cursive shapes in question are typical of "the last decades before the Roman destruction of Jerusalem."[+] In addition, the presence of both cursive and formal lettering in the same inscription is not by itself sufficient to establish the presence of two hands, especially in an ossuary inscription. Variations in spelling and forms of letters are common in these inscriptions, because they were usually written at the time of secondary burial by members of the immediate family within the confines of the family burial cave. In such circumstances, variations are to be expected. Finally, the content of the inscription is also typical of Jewish ossuary inscriptions from the Early Roman period in Jerusalem. It identifies the deceased in the way that Jews of this region and period customarily identified themselves: "X son of Y." On the whole, then, this ossuary could hardly be a more typical Early Roman Jewish artifact. If not for the constellation of names in the inscription, its authenticity would be unquestioned, and it would have to be regarded as a generally unremarkable specimen.

The constellation of names in the inscription is, however, anything but unremarkable. "James, son of Joseph, brother of Jesus" configures a set of relationships which coincides with the present state of our knowledge about one of the more important figures in primitive Christianity. Appearing in such early Christian documents as the books of Matthew, Mark, Acts, 1 Corinthians, and Galatians, and outside the New Testament in the Gospel according to the Hebrews (quoted by Jerome in *de Vir. Ill. 2*), James is remembered as both the brother of Jesus and as the leader of the earliest Christian movement in Jerusalem. Josephus mentions that "James, the brother of Jesus" was convicted and condemned by the Sanhedrin around the year 62 C.E. (*Ant.* 20.200). The coincidence of these historical data with the names in the inscription led André Lemaire to argue that this otherwise ordinary ossuary was "very probably" the burial container of a prominent figure in earliest Christianity. On that basis he described the ossuary as "the first epigraphic mention—from about 63 C.E.—of Jesus of Nazareth."

Lemaire's analysis is careful and cogent, but there are unfortunately three significant problems with it. The first has to do with statistics. He draws upon the known frequencies of the names Ya`acob, Yosef, and Yeshua in order to estimate the likelihood that a Jewish male in Jerusalem during the first century C.E. might have been named Ya`acob, with a father Yosef and a brother Yeshua. He correctly notes that these three names are among the most common for Jewish males in this region and period. After examining inscriptions from across early Roman Palestine, Rachel Hachlili calculated the rate of occurrence for the name Yosef at 14%, Yeshua at 9%, and Ya`acob at 2% of the total of Jewish male names in this region and period.[5] Levi Rahmani's study of ossuary inscriptions has produced similar frequencies.[6] On this basis, Lemaire computed the statistical probability that this particular constellation of names and relationships would occur in one Jewish male during the first century C.E. in Jerusalem. Assuming that the average Jewish male had two brothers, the resulting figure was a mere 0.05 percent. In other words, a Jewish male named Ya`acob, with father Yosef and brother Yeshua, was about one in two thousand. Correlating this percentage with current scholarly population estimates for first-century C.E. Jerusalem, Lemaire reasoned that "in Jerusalem during the two generations before 70 C.E., there were probably about 20 people who could be called 'James/Jacob son of Joseph brother of Jesus.'"[7] Here we encounter the first problem with a statistical analysis of this artifact: it actually establishes a very low probability that the inscription refers to James, the brother of Jesus of Nazareth. As a matter of statistical probability, any one of those twenty or so men named Ya`acob could have been the one whose bones were gathered in this ossuary, and only one of them was James, brother of Jesus of Nazareth. One out of twenty equals five percent, a very low level of probability which does not make it "very probable that this is the ossuary of the James in the New Testament."

Clearly the weight of Lemaire's argument on behalf of this ossuary and its inscription does not lie with statistical probabilities. It rests instead upon his evaluation of the significance of the closing phrase, "ahui diYeshua." Lemaire believes that the addition of this unusual phrase signified something special about the brother Yeshua: "The mention of the brother probably means that the brother had a particular role, either in taking responsibility for the burial, or more generally, because the brother was known, and the deceased had a special connection with him." As we have already seen in chapter 1, it is indeed very common for the father's name to appear alongside the name of the deceased in an ossuary inscription, and quite rare for a brother's name to appear there. We have also seen that in some cases, ossuary inscriptions include information about the deceased which family members regarded as socially or religiously significant. The inclusion of a brother's name therefore might be due to the fact that, in the eyes of the family, the brother had particular social or religious standing. Here, however, we encounter the second problem with the argument that this inscription refers to the brother of Jesus of Nazareth: the mention of a brother's name in an ossuary inscription did not necessarily carry any special social or religious significance. There could also be other reasons for including a brother's name. In the corpus of ossuary inscriptions surveyed by Levi Rahmani, for example, there is an inscription which has exactly the same form as that on the "James" ossuary: "X, son of Y, brother of Z." This inscription, scrawled on the side of an ossuary found in a tomb on Mt. Scopus, reads "Shimi bar `siah 'ahui Hanin," or "Shimi son of Asiah, brother of Hanin."[8] In this inscription there is no apparent social or religious significance to the inclusion of the brother's name, and no reason for an archaeologist to construct one. Rahmani comments drily: "In certain cases, relatives found it important to indicate a sibling relationship in addition to a patronymic."[9] Among the possible reasons for including the name of a brother, a rather mundane and practical one lies close at hand. A typical Jewish burial cave of the first century C.E. held the remains of multiple generations of family members, and names were often repeated across generations. The purpose of ossuary inscriptions was to identify the deceased. A brother's name may have been included, then, for no more serious purpose than to differentiate between a grandson and a grandfather or between second cousins. Since the original archaeological context of this ossuary is unknown, such mundane explanations cannot be ruled out.

At this point we have come upon the third and most serious weakness in Lemaire's argument, and it is a deficiency for which he himself bears no responsibility: the archaeological context of this artifact has been irretrievably lost. In the absence of such a context, observed and recorded by careful excavators, it will never be possible to evaluate this artifact with certainty. The "burial box of James" came to light through suspicious circumstances that are still clouded in mystery. The location and date of its discovery will never be known. As a result, interpreters of this ossuary are forced to rely upon guesswork, calculation, and imagination rather than archaeological data. There are no field notebooks, excavation reports, or analyses of the finds—only statistical probabilities, laboratory examinations, and articles in the media. Lemaire has made the best of a bad situation, but it must be pointed out that the situation could have been much different. If the looters who first discovered the tomb and sold this ossuary on the antiquities market had contacted archaeological authorities instead, then this artifact would have been recovered through a controlled excavation. Questions about its provenance and significance would be answerable with much greater confidence. Excavators would have drawn a plan of the tomb, recording not only the precise find spot for this ossuary, but also those of all the other ossuaries which would have been found with it. Some of those ossuaries would have been inscribed, and the names therein could have been interpreted in the light of each other. The excavators would have consulted with trained epigraphers (possibly including André Lemaire) in order to produce an analysis and report on all these inscriptions. Human skeletal remains contained in the ossuary would have been carefully preserved for analysis by physical anthropologists, who would have established the age and gender of the person (or persons) whose bones were collected within. Perhaps the cause of death might even have been evident in the skeletal remains. Reports on the pottery and lamps found in the tomb would have added further detail to the archaeological context. Under such conditions excavators have at times been able to establish that a particular tomb was related to this or that prominent historical figure from antiquity. But in such cases everything depends upon information gleaned from the archaeological context, for (as field archaeologists know) the context of an artifact often provides as much or more information than the artifact itself. In the case of this ossuary, however, that information is gone forever. When looters picked up this ossuary from the shelf or niche in which it lay, dumped the bones inside onto the floor of the tomb, and sold it to an antiquities dealer, they permanently obliterated an irreplaceable trove of information about its background. Because of their actions we will never be able to know what we would like to know.

Can anything at all be said with confidence about this ossuary and its inscription? Yes, a little. Clearly it has all the physical characteristics of a typical Jewish ossuary from the early Roman period in Jerusalem. Its size, shape, decoration, and inscription are all consistent with the characteristic features of containers for secondary burial from that time and place. The burden of proof would lie very heavily upon anyone who would want to argue that this artifact does not come from early Roman Jerusalem. It is therefore reasonable to believe that this ossuary once contained the bones of a Jewish man from first-century Jerusalem who was called "Ya`acob son of Yosef." It is also reasonable to believe that this Ya`acob had a brother named Yeshua. Given the limits of our knowledge about the background of this ossuary, however, it is not reasonable to believe that this Ya`acob was the leader of the earliest Christian communities in Jerusalem and the brother of Jesus of Nazareth. Nor is it reasonable to connect this ossuary in any way with Jesus of Nazareth. The names in the inscription are ordinary Jewish names from first-century Jerusalem, as is the constellation of relationships between father, son, and brother. In the absence of reliable information drawn from the archaeological context of this artifact, assertions that it is related to Jesus of Nazareth have to be characterized as imaginative, speculative, and sensationalistic. As a matter of serious archaeological discussion, they must be ruled out of the question.

The history of the relationship between archaeology and New Testament studies during the second half of the twentieth century already includes a series of episodes in which scholars have become fascinated with finds that appeared to be related to events or people mentioned in the biblical text. From the Talpioth ossuaries to the "Jesus boat," from the crucified man of Giv'at ha-Mivtar to the "Caiaphas" tomb, the guild of New Testament scholarship has occasionally allowed itself to be tantalized by the prospect of archaeological confirmation for the New Testament narrative. This book has been written in the hope that it might in some measure contribute to a more comprehensive relationship between the disciplines of field archaeology and textual studies, by suggesting how much there is to be gained from a more substantial conversation between them. The social and cultural context of the New Testament is illumined more clearly by many ordinary archaeological finds than by a single sensational discovery. Louis Robert's famous dictum about inscriptions applies equally well to archaeological finds: "If you see one, you have seen none; if you see a thousand, you have seen one."

By the way, this book has also been written in order to make the case that the primitive Christians in early Roman Palestine buried their dead in the same manner as did other Jews in that place and time. It is ironic that if by some chance the "burial box of James" did in fact belong to the brother of Jesus of Nazareth, it would provide material confirmation for the principal assertion of this book.

NOTES TO CONCLUSION

1. "Jesus Inscription on Stone May Be Earliest Ever Found," *New York Times*, 22 October 2002, A14.

2. André Lemaire, "Burial Box of James the Brother of Jesus: Earliest Archaeological Evidence of Jesus Found in Jerusalem," *Biblical Archaeology Review* 28, no. 6 (2002): 33.

3. Eric M. Meyers, quoted in "Experts Question Authenticity of Bone Box for 'Brother of Jesus,'" *New York Times*, 3 December 2002, F3.

4. Lemaire, "Burial Box of James the Brother of Jesus," 28.

5. Rachel Hachlili, "Names and Nicknames of Jews in Second-Temple Times," *Eretz Israel* 17 (1984): 188–211.

6. Levi Rahmani, *A Catalogue of Jewish Ossuaries in the Collections of the State of Israel* (Jerusalem: Israel Exploration Society, 1994), 13.

7. Lemaire, "Burial Box of James the Brother of Jesus," 33.

8. Rahmani, *A Catalogue of Jewish Ossuaries*, #570.

9. Ibid., 15.

Select Bibliography

Bloch-Smith, Elizabeth. *Judahite Burial Practices and Beliefs about the Dead.* Journal for the Study of the Old Testament: Supplement Series 123. Sheffield: Sheffield Academic Press, 1992.

Boyarin, Daniel. *Dying for God: Martyrdom and the Making of Christianity and Judaism.* Stanford: Stanford University Press, 1999.

Hertz, Robert. *Death and the Right Hand.* Translated by Rodney and Claudia Needham. Aberdeen: The University Press, 1960.

Kloppenborg, John S. *Excavating Q.* Philadelphia: Fortress, 2000.

Metcalf, Peter and Richard Huntington. *Celebrations of Death: The Anthropology of Mortuary Ritual.* 2d ed. Cambridge: Cambridge University Press, 1992.

Morris, Ian. *Burial and Ancient Society.* Cambridge: Cambridge University Press, 1987.

———. *Death-Ritual and Social Structures in Classical Antiquity.* Cambridge: Cambridge University Press, 1992.

Rahmani, Levi. *A Catalogue of Jewish Ossuaries in the Collections of the State of Israel.* Jerusalem: Israel Antiquities Authority, 1994.

Reed, Jonathan L. *Archaeology and the Galilean Jesus: A Re-examination of the Evidence.* Harrisburg, Pa.: Trinity Press International, 2000

Smith, Jonathan Z. *Drudgery Divine: On the Comparison of Early Christianities and the Religions of Late Antiquity.* Chicago: University of Chicago Press, 1990.

van Gennep, Arnold. *The Rites of Passage.* Translated by M. B. Vizedom and G. L. Caffee. Chicago: University of Chicago Press, 1960.

Index